For Everything A Season

75 Blessings for Daily Life

For Everything A Season

75 Blessings for Daily Life

by the Nilsen Family

Zion Publishing
Des Moines, Iowa

FOR EVERYTHING A SEASON
75 Blessings for Daily Life

Written by the Nilsen Family:

**Mary Ylvisaker Nilsen and Roy Nilsen, Per and Mary Nilsen, Kai and Patricia Nilsen,
Linnea Nilsen Capshaw and Daniel Capshaw, Solveig and Peter Nilsen-Goodin, Erika Nilsen and David Devine.**

Unless otherwise noted, Scripture texts are from or adapted from the New Revised Standard Version of the Bible,
copyright 1989, by the Division of Christian Education of the National Council of the Churches of Christ in the USA
and used by permission. All rights reserved.

Cover and Illustrations by
Kristi Ylvisaker, Sogndal, Norway

Page Design and Layout by
Karen Beach, Red Clover Graphic Design, Des Moines, Iowa

For ordering information, contact

**Zion Publishing
1500 Crown Colony Court, Suite 540
Des Moines, Iowa 50315-1073**

ISBN 0-9627147-1-2
Library of Congress Catalogue Card Number: 99-93976

Printed in the United States of America

To children everywhere —

especially Bjorn, Kristian, Anders, Annika, Leif, and Hanson

Table of Contents

Preface   viii
Introduction   ix

SEASONS OF THE DAY

Blessing for the Morning   2
Blessing for Meals   3
Blessing for the Evening   4

SEASONS OF THE YEAR

Blessing for Birthdays   6
Blessing for New Year's Eve   7
Blessing for Martin Luther King, Jr. Day   8
Blessing for Valentine's Day   9
Blessing for Mother's Day and Father's Day   10

Blessing for Memorial Day   11
Blessing for the Fourth of July   12
Blessing for Labor Day   13
Blessing for the New School Year   14
Blessing for Halloween Eve
    of All Saints' Day   15
Blessing for Thanksgiving Day   16

Blessing for Heritage Holidays   17
Blessing for the Changing of the Seasons   18

SEASONS OF OUR LIVES

Blessing Our Developmental Milestones   20
Blessing Our Adolescent Body Changes   21
Blessing upon Getting a Driver's License   22
Blessing Our Graduations and Achievements   23
Blessing for Those Leaving Home   24
Blessing for Those Traveling   25
Blessing for New Beginnings   26

Blessing for a New Home   27
Blessing for the Single Life   28
Blessing for Times of Loss and/or Gratitude   29
Blessing for a New Pet   30
Blessing for the Death of a Pet   31

Blessing of Encouragement for Care-Givers   32
Blessing for an Ill Friend or Family Member   33
Blessing before Surgery   34
Blessing for Those Struggling with Infertility   35
Blessing for Times of Disappointment
    with Ourselves   36
Blessing for Times of Weariness
    and Muddling Through   37
Blessing of Encouragement in Times
    of Prejudice or Discrimination   38

Blessing for Moving Out and Moving On   39
Blessing during a Job Transition   40
Blessing for the Empty Nest   41
Blessing Our Mid-Life Body Changes   42
Blessing for Retirement   43
Blessing Our Loss of Independence   44

SEASONS OF OUR RELATIONSHIPS

Blessing of Friendship 46

Blessing for Revealing Our Hidden Selves 47

Blessing for Forgiveness and Reconciliation 48

Blessing for a Reunion of Family or Friends 49

Blessing of Intentional Relationships 50

Blessing of a Marriage 51

Blessing of a Pregnancy 52

Blessing after a Stillbirth or Miscarriage 53

Blessing of a Birth or Adoption 54

Blessing of Wedding Anniversaries 55

Blessing for Important Conversations 56

Blessing after the Ending or Changing
of a Relationship 57

Blessing for a Blended Family 58

Blessing for Letting Go of a Loved One
Near Death 59

Blessing and Sending after a Funeral 60

Blessing for the Disposition of Ashes 61

Blessing for the Anniversary of a Death 62

Blessing for Discerning Our Vocation and
Other Significant Choices 69

Blessing the Discovery of Our Spiritual Gifts 70

Blessing for Commitment or Recommitment
to Jesus Christ 71

Blessing of Closure When Leaving
a Congregation or Group 72

Blessing for Times of Struggle, Doubt
and Despair 73

Blessing for Protection against Evil 74

SEASONS OF THE CHURCH YEAR

Blessing for Advent 76

Blessing for The Twelve Days of
Christmas 77

Blessing for Epiphany 78

Blessing for Lent 79

Blessing for Easter 80

Blessing for Pentecost 81

SEASONS OF THE CHRISTIAN LIFE

Blessing for Baptismal Anniversaries 64

Blessing for Entry into Church School 65

Blessing for Receiving Your First Bible 66

Blessing for First Communion 67

Blessing for Confirmation 68

APPENDIX

Advent and Lenten Texts 83

Song: "As You Go on Your Way" 84

Prayers 84

Preface

For everything there is a season.

As the bleakness of a Minnesota winter turns to lush spring growth, so the rhythms of our lives are marked by transforming ritual. A great-grandfather's veined, weathered hand gently surrounds the tiny, tender hand of his newly born great-grandchild, and endings and beginnings are bound together as one.

A teenager, devastated over the loss of a relationship, buries her head in her mother's lap. The same mother, just hours before, had been the target of this daughter's adolescent rage — and the cycle of dependence and independence comes full circle again.

A daughter glides down the aisle to meet her new husband as tears falling from her parents' eyes mix the joy of new beginnings with the sorrow of endings.

Some of the rituals that give rhythm to our lives are intentional on our part — patterns that shape our days like a morning cup of coffee and the paper, a prayer before a meal, a book before bed. Some are simply movements in God's great symphony of life — patterns of day and night, growth and decay, summer and winter, life and death.

Each gives shape and order to our lives just as the tide molds the shifting sands of the shoreline, at times pounding away leaving debris on the shore, and at other times gently, imperceptibly carrying off the old and reshaping the new.

This book is a family project, conceived by a family who, over the years, discovered the power of ritual.

Our family created sacred, holy space each night of Advent (the season before Christmas) by lighting the Advent candles and singing Advent songs. We also found many ways to make the season of Lent (the weeks before Easter) different from the rest of the year. We all look back on those times as moments of grace during which our love of God, our connection with each other, and our sense of awe and wonder were formed and deepened. Through the years we have incorporated both old and new rituals into our new families.

We have become increasingly aware of many people of faith who yearn for some sense of the sacred in the midst of very hectic lives. However, they simply do not know what to do or how to do it. This book is one response to the question, "How can I make both the ordinary and the special events of my life and the lives of those I care about more intentionally sacred?"

The hope our family has for you, as you begin or continue this common journey of faith, is that you will discover the profound joy and hope of this God who can bring calm in the midst of chaos, turn our mourning into dancing, and transform our everyday interactions in time and place into holy moments of timeless grace.

For everything there is a season.

The Nilsen Family

Introduction

BEGINNING TO USE THIS BOOK

1) Look through the list of blessings in the Table of Contents and choose one that seems appropriate for the occasion.

2) Read through the blessing in its entirety before you begin. Occasionally there will be word choices you must make. These words will be separated by a / mark — for instance, his/her. Circle the appropriate word ahead of time so your reading will be smooth.

3) Choose a quiet space in your home and set out designated objects according to the directions in the blessing.

4) Make copies of the blessing, if necessary.
   When appropriate, ask others to share leadership.

5) Set aside plenty of time. Many of the blessings can be done in 5-10 minutes. Others need more time, based on the number of people present and the depth of reflection.

SETTING THE TONE OF THE BLESSING RITUALS

The tone of these blessings varies depending on the event (a birthday can be joyous and fun, whereas the death of a pet will be much more somber). However the spirit under-girding these blessings is always one of grace, freedom, and joy, not of rigidity or coercion.

This is especially important with children. All children should be encouraged to be part of a blessing, but if a child refuses to participate, let him or her be. Some of the most wonderful moments happen when the blessings do not go as prescribed or planned.

The point of these blessings is not to create one more thing to add to a busy day, one more thing to check off your list. These blessings need to be approached as a gift, a time set apart for restoration from the busy day, a moment when you intentionally open yourself to God, claiming divine presence and love in your daily life.

EXPLAINING THE BLESSING RITUALS

Preparation

The space you choose is important. Ideally, it should be uncluttered and quiet, so people are not distracted. Many family blessings can happen around the kitchen or dining room table or in the living room. Other more private blessings need a quiet corner of the house where beautiful objects, spiritual writings, candles, or other sensory objects can help you set aside the cares of the day and enter into holy space. Dimming or turning off lights is often helpful in creating this sense of God's presence with us.

Each blessing asks that you gather certain objects. It is helpful to prepare in advance by having frequently used objects, such as candles, on hand. Before beginning the blessing, eliminate as much noise as possible — turn off the TV or sound system, disconnect the phone, close doors or windows . . .

Read through the blessing so you know what is needed. If the blessing has options, choose the one that will work best for you. Then make all other changes in language or form so it will fit your occasion. These blessings are meant to be suggestions or guides that can be adapted in any way appropriate to the situation.

Welcome

Each blessing begins with a welcome, an invitation into sacred time and space. Generally, one person will hold this book and lead the blessing, or leadership can be shared. Do what works for you.

Opening Prayer and Text

All the blessings begin with prayer and words from the Bible. If you prefer using your own words in prayer, feel free to do so.

Reflection

Each blessing calls for a time of reflection — thinking, talking or writing about your feelings and experiences. It is a time to let God use the raw materials of your life — particularly those moments of joy or sorrow, of peace or fear, of love or anger — as teaching moments. If you are alone, write down your thoughts and feelings in a journal. If with a group, ask those present to share only what they are comfortable sharing. No one should be put on the spot or manipulated to say more than he or she wants to say. All responses are to be received with respect and openness.

Ritual Action

After the reflection, most rituals contain some ritual action such as lighting candles or passing the blessing cup. Some of the reflections and ritual actions contain two options. The first option is generally shorter and simpler. Choose the option you think will work best for you or your family/friends. Take into consideration the time available and how comfortable people are with certain questions or techniques.

Singing

Individuals and families vary dramatically in how comfortable they are with singing. If you are a singing person or family, add as many hymns or songs as you like to any of these blessings. Music is a gift from God that helps us sense the holy in our midst. However, if you are not comfortable singing,when there are songs suggested, simply read the words.

There is one blessing song, *As You Go on Your Way*, printed on p. 84. We encourage you to memorize the words and sing or say them at the end of any of these blessings. You may also want to have sacred background music playing during certain blessings.

Blessing

Each blessing ritual ends with a blessing, a hope, a prayerful desire that God will be with us and help us as we go on with our lives. You are also encouraged to close any of these blessings with the Lord's Prayer, the Serenity Prayer (see p. 84), or any other common prayer.

SPECIAL INSTRUCTIONS:

1. The Blessing Cup

Passing the blessing cup is an ancient tradition, predating the practice of Christian communion by hundreds of years. Recently, it has been reclaimed by many religious groups as a way of celebrating God's action in our lives and the importance of others to our well-being. You are encouraged to designate a special cup as your blessing cup. When a ritual action calls for a blessing cup, take that cup and fill it with water, juice, or wine. Set it on the table.

Most of the ritual actions simply ask you to speak a word of blessing to the person next to you or to one special person in the group, take a sip from the cup, and pass it on. Use common sense with this ritual action. If people in the group have colds or other infectious diseases, be sure to wipe the lip of the cup before passing it on or have separate small cups for each person. Be sensitive to those in the group who cannot or should not drink wine. Fill the cup with juice or water instead.

2. Candles

God says in Genesis 1, *Let there be light.* The Gospel of John speaks of Jesus as the light shining in the darkness. The symbolism of light permeates Christian tradition. Many ritual actions in this book ask you to light candles — often one large candle and several small ones. If possible, reduce the other light in the room, so as to create a space where candle light flickers and glows, casting shadows and creating a sense of mystery and awe in the room. Blow out the candles to mark the end of the blessing.

Be ready to do a blessing at any time by having on hand tall candles that have an exposed wick. Also have small candles — either votive candles or tea candles (in small metal cups). These can be purchased at most grocery or drug stores. Be cautious when using candles with children so they will not burn themselves.

3. The Begging Bowl

By using the begging bowl, Christians are reclaiming a practice from the Middle Ages when monks would go out in the morning with an empty bowl, believing that God, working through other people, would put in their bowl all the food they needed for the day. We expand this idea beyond physical needs and link it to the Lord's Prayer — *Give us this day our daily bread.* By holding out your begging bowl, you are acknowledging dependence on your Creator for everything and trusting that the God who loves you will give you what you need that day.

Choose a small bowl as your special begging bowl, perhaps a wooden or pottery one, and set it aside for the ritual action.

4. Deep Breathing

One option in many of the ritual actions is to take time to deep breathe. Breathing meditation is a technique used by many Christians through the centuries for clearing the mind and becoming present in time and space, open to the Spirit of God. It can be done very simply.

Close your eyes and breathe in through your nose, letting the air fill your body to the base of your abdomen. Then let the air out through your mouth. There should be little or no movement in your shoulders or chest, only the movement in and out of your abdomen.

Concentrate on your breath, feeling it come in and go out, come in and go out. You might want to say a holy word (**Jesus, Lord, peace . . .**) or phrase (**"Lord Jesus Christ, have mercy on me," "The Lord is my shepherd, I shall not want". . .**) over and over again while you breathe. Continue until you feel centered and at peace.

5. The "Squeeze Prayer"

Several ritual actions suggest this form of prayer. It is simply a time when those gathered hold hands. One person begins praying and, when finished, squeezes the hand of the next person. That person can then pray or simply pass the prayer on by squeezing the hand of the person on his or her other side. In this way, no one feels pressured to pray aloud, and it is clear when the praying is over.

6. Making the Sign of the Cross

Through this ancient ritual action, Christians claim for their lives the power of God the Creator, Jesus the Redeemer, and the Holy Spirit the Comforter. In some blessings you are asked to make the sign of the cross by placing the tips of your fingers of one hand on your forehead, then moving them to the center of your chest, then to the left shoulder, and then the right.

In other blessings you make the sign of the cross on your forehead or the forehead of another with water or oil. It is common practice to use your first two fingers for water and your thumb for oil. The use of water recalls baptismal water and covenant. The use of oil recalls the ancient practice of anointing for healing and protection.

7. Visualization

Several ritual actions contain an option that asks you to visualize something. This means simply closing your eyes and imagining or putting a picture of something in your mind and holding it there. For instance, if a person is ill, remember a time when that person was well. Put that image in your mind and hold it there. Or the visualization might be more active, asking you to imagine something happening (like the light of Christ moving into a dark place). The point is to keep your mind focused on one thing.

8. Keeping a Journal

Many of the blessings have a suggestion for writing in a journal, particularly if you are doing the blessing by yourself. There is deep power in writing. Some say we discover what we are thinking by reading what we have written. Yet most people have blocks when it comes to writing, fearing that their spelling might be wrong or their grammar inaccurate or someone might find what they have written and judge them for it.

Writing in a journal is a way to free you from those anxieties and release deep thoughts and feelings. No one will check your spelling, no one cares about your grammar — in fact, you are encouraged to write in a stream of consciousness with no regard to grammar or sentence structure. Simply write whatever comes to mind whether or not it makes sense or is well-written. And remember, you are always free to tear up anything you write so no one else will ever read it.

In all the reflections where you are asked to write, there are questions guiding your response. It might be helpful to imagine you are writing a letter and address your words to God or another person with whom you feel free to share.

For some it is easier to begin with their feelings, asking, "What is on my heart?" For others it is easier to begin with their thoughts, asking, "What is on my mind?" Do whatever works best for you, but try to write about both thoughts and feelings. Keep in mind that feelings are neither right nor wrong, good nor bad. They just are. No feeling is too silly or petty or negative to write about. The same is true for the ideas that float through your mind.

Remember, there is no wrong way to keep a journal. It is personal and private. The more free and experienced you become with the practice, the more helpful it will become to you.

9. Memorization of the Bible Text

The things we memorize, those sayings or concepts that end up in our subconscious, affect the way we think and act. It becomes very important, then, what we memorize. If you are doing blessing rituals for and with children, you might want to be especially intentional about making memorization of the Bible text a part of the blessing. Children learn very quickly. Have them say each phrase of the verse several times. Then put it all together. Make a game of it. Repeat it from time to time. Soon it will become part of the child's memory bank, affecting how that child thinks and acts.

For everything there is a season.

As you become more comfortable with these blessing rituals, begin to introduce them into new occasions and in other relationships.

For example, gather friends for a house blessing, invite family members to participate in one of the holiday blessings, encourage your congregation to celebrate spiritual gifts, or explore ways to adapt a blessing for your work place. Soon a deep sense of the sacred will begin to permeate your daily life and you will know that your life is held securely in the hollow of God's hand.

For everything there is a season.

SEASONS OF THE DAY

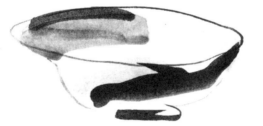

Blessing for the Morning

PREPARATION Find a quiet time and space either alone or with others. This may mean getting up 15 minutes early. For option 2, have your begging bowl* at hand. Add your own daily devotional if you have one.

WELCOME
For everything there is a season,
and a time for every matter under heaven.

Welcome to this day that the Lord has made;
let us rejoice and be glad in it! Psalm 118:24

BIBLE TEXT
Let me hear of your steadfast love in the morning,
for in you I put my trust. Teach me the way
I should go, for to you I lift up my soul.
Psalm 143:8

REFLECTION
OPTION 1 —Pray this prayer,
My God and my Life,
I lift up each part of my day to you.
(Name them and place them in God's hands.)
I lift up the people I will encounter.
(Name as many as you know and place them in God's hands.)
Help me believe that your grace is sufficient for the day,
for in you I put my trust. Amen

OPTION 2 — Read any other daily devotional you use. Spend some time deep breathing. Then visualize* your day. Go through it as you imagine it will unfold. Place each event and each person into God's open hand. Think specifically about those points of frustration and need in your life. Hold your begging bowl and pray this prayer,
Gracious God, give me this day all I need for the day. Amen.

RITUAL ACTION
Make the sign of the cross* and say these words,
I can do all things through Christ who strengthens me.
(Philippians 4:13)

*For more information see the Introduction.

BLESSING
May I be reminded of your steadfast love throughout the day, for in you I put my trust. Amen

Blessing for Meals

PREPARATION The psalmist in the text for this blessing speaks of the Lord as one who prepares a table for us, as a homemaker who prepares and serves food, as one who delights in gathering people around a table and feeding them. There is sacredness in the simple act of preparing food and gathering people to eat together. Yet, we often allow the hectic pace of life to keep us from taking time to make eating together a sacred moment. With a little forward planning and a little time, you can change the spirit with which eating is done in your home or life. Have those planning to eat gather at the table at the same time. Before eating, ask for quiet.

WELCOME
For everything there is a season,
and a time for every matter under heaven.
Welcome to this time for celebrating the
gift of food and nourishment
provided by God.

PRAYER
(On those days when you have only
a few minutes, go directly to the prayer possibilities.)
Provider God, as the rain and sun bring refreshment and growth to the natural world, so also these gifts of food are the sustenance and nourishment for our bodies. Help us to recognize that all these simple gifts come from your gracious hand. Amen

BIBLE TEXT
You prepare a table before me . . . Psalm 23:5

O give thanks to the Lord who is good,
whose steadfast love endures forever. Psalm 106:1

RITUAL PRAYER POSSIBILITIES
(Choose one or use one of your own.)
Come Lord Jesus, be our guest, and let thy gifts to us be blessed. Amen (Traditional prayer)

God is great. God is good. Let us thank God for our food. By God's hand we all are fed. Give us Lord our daily bread. Amen (Traditional prayer)

Accept our gratitude, O Lord, for all the blessings that you give. Direct and guide our daily paths, and teach us how to live. In Jesus' name we pray. Amen (Traditional prayer)

Gracious God, thank you for the food before us, the friends beside us, the love between us, and your presence among us. Amen (Traditional prayer)

The eyes of all look to you, and you give them their food in due season. You open your hand, and satisfy the desire of every living thing. Amen (Psalm 145:15-16)

BLESSING
May these gifts of food be strength for our bodies as the Word of God is strength for our lives. Amen
(Say this after the prayer or at the end of the meal.)

Blessing for the Evening

PREPARATION Find a quiet time and place, either alone or with others. There are many options in this blessing. Choose those that work best for you.

WELCOME

For everything there is a season,
and a time for every matter under heaven.
Welcome to this time for celebrating the day that
the Lord has made.

BIBLE TEXT

It is good to give thanks to the Lord, to sing praises to your name . . . to declare your steadfast love in the morning and your faithfulness by night. Psalm 92:1-2

REFLECTION

OPTION 1 (with those gathered)
Share the part of the day you liked
the best and the time when you were
the most frustrated, angry, hurt . . .

OPTION 2 (if you are alone)
Take an inventory of your day. Use these sentence
starters to write in a journal* or think about:
I am thankful to God for . . . I confess that I disappointed or
failed myself, others, and/or God in these ways . . . I remember
the people, places, and events that need my prayers . . .

RITUAL ACTION

OPTION 1—Make the sign of the cross* in remembrance of
your baptism, saying, *Create in me a clean heart, O God, and
put a new and right spirit within me* (Psalm 51:10).

OPTION 2 —Spend time deep breathing,* letting all thoughts
of the day float out of your mind and into the care
of your Creator.

PRAYER

OPTION 1 — Now I lay me down to sleep. I pray the Lord
your child to keep. May your love guard me through the night
and wake me with the morning light. This I ask for Jesus'
sake. Amen (Traditional prayer)

OPTION 2 — Go around the room praying the Lord's Prayer
for the person next to you. If you are alone, pray it for each
person you care about, including yourself.
(Name)'s Father/Creator in heaven, hallowed be your name,
your kingdom come, your will be done in (name)'s life as in
heaven. Give (name) all she/he needs for today, especially: (use
words of your own). Forgive (name) his/her sins, as (name)
forgives those who sin against him/her. Save (name) from the
time of trial and deliver him/her from evil. For the kingdom,
the power and the glory are yours, now and forever. Amen

*For more information see the Introduction.

BLESSING

May God grant to all refreshing sleep. Amen

Seasons of the Year

Blessing for Birthdays

PREPARATION For option 1 — a gathering of family and friends — make a cake or some other treat. Place candles on it. Decorate the room using balloons, streamers or other festive decor. Have simple gifts ready. For option 2 — celebrating your birthday alone — find pictures of yourself from the past year and place them on a table. Light a candle.*

WELCOME
For everything there is a season,
and a time for every matter under heaven.
Welcome to this time of joy and thankfulness for life!

PRAYER
God of our days and our years, thank you for birth and for life. May my/our heart(s) be filled with joy, as you rejoiced on the day (name) was born. Amen

BIBLE TEXT
For it was you who formed my inward parts; you knit me together in my mother's womb. I praise you, for I am fearfully and wonderfully made. Psalm 139:13-14

REFLECTION
OPTION 1 — Have each person in the room think of and say something affirming to the birthday person.

OPTION 2 — Reflect on the many blessings of the past year of your life. What were your most meaningful events and most difficult challenges? Dream about the possibilities for the coming year. Write your responses in a journal.*

RITUAL ACTION
OPTION 1 — Sing "Happy Birthday," blow out the candles, feast on the prepared food. As the birthday person opens gifts, if he or she is old enough, suggest this response: **Thank you for this gift, and thank you for the gift of _____ you bring to my life.** (This is an opportunity for the birthday person to return an affirming statement to each guest.)

OPTION 2 — Close your eyes and spend time deep breathing.* Visualize* God's hands before you. Then place in God's hands all your hopes and dreams for the coming year. Ask God to shape those hopes and dreams in accordance with God's hopes for you. Relax into God's loving care.

*For more information see the introduction.

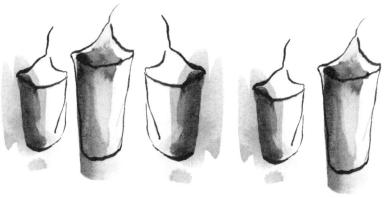

BLESSING
May this year be rich in blessings and peace for (name), whom God has wonderfully made and continues to sustain. Amen.

Blessing for New Year's Eve

PREPARATION New Year's Eve became a celebration and religious feast in 1582 when Pope Gregory XIII developed the Gregorian Calendar. Prior to that, the new year began in March. Set out the past year's calendar or date book along with next year's calendar or date book. Light a candle* and fill a blessing cup.*

WELCOME

For everything there is a season,
and a time for every matter under heaven.
Welcome to this time for honoring the past year
and looking forward to the future with hope.

PRAYER

God of new beginnings, thank you for this past year — the joyful moments and the growing moments, the celebrations and the defeats. Give to all the strength to entrust this new year to you, knowing that with you there is a future filled with hope. Amen

BIBLE TEXT

For surely I know the plans I have for you, says the Lord, plans for your welfare and not for harm, to give you a future with hope. Jeremiah 29:11

REFLECTION

New Year's Eve is a celebration of the old and the new, the past and the future. Share or write in a journal* about the past year. These sentence starters may be helpful:
One of the many blessings of this past year was . . . One of the disappointments of this past year was . . . One of the ways I have changed over the past year is . . .

Now think ahead to the new year and complete the following sentences: **One fear I have for this year is . . . One hope I have for this year is . . .**

RITUAL ACTION

OPTION 1 (if you are alone)
Hold the blessing cup and say, **Trusting in God's purpose for my life, I have hope for the future.** Drink from the cup.

OPTION 2 (for use with a group)
Pass the blessing cup, saying,
(Name), God gives you a future with hope.

*For more information see the Introduction.

BLESSING

May this new year be filled with blessings and with grace, and may we always have hope for tomorrow. Amen

Blessing for Martin Luther King, Jr. Day

PREPARATION In 1983, the third Monday of January was set aside to honor the slain civil rights activist and advocate of biblically based non-violence, Reverend Dr. Martin Luther King, Jr. It is a time to recall and reclaim his vision of freedom and justice for all peoples. Fill a blessing cup* with drinking water and place it on a table. If possible, find a copy of Dr. King's *'I Have a Dream'* speech and set this, along with paper and pencils/pens, on the table.

WELCOME

For everything there is a season,
and a time for every matter under heaven.
Welcome to this time for inspiring
our dreams for a better world.

PRAYER

Holy Spirit of Truth, make our hearts burn with passion
for love and justice. Give us the courage
of the prophets and saints who have
gone before us. Amen

BIBLE TEXT

Let justice roll down like waters
and righteousness like an
ever-flowing stream.
Amos 5:24

. . . and what does the Lord
require of you but to do justice,
and to love kindness, and to
walk humbly with your God.
Micah 6:8

REFLECTION

If you have it, read Dr. King's *'I Have a Dream'* speech. Take some time to think about, write in a journal* about, or draw some of your dreams for a more just and peaceful world, using the theme:
I have a dream that . . . All who wish may share their dreams. Then share or write in a journal about concrete ways you can make your dream a reality.

RITUAL ACTION

As each person takes the blessing cup and drinks, others say,
May God fill you with courage, (name).
When all have finished, one person says,
May this water of justice make our dreams come alive
for all God's people.

SONG OPTIONS

Sing any song that inspires dreams, hope and courage in you for the ongoing struggle for freedom and justice.
(Suggestions: *Lift Ev'ry Voice and Sing,*
We Shall Overcome, Here I Am, Lord)

*For more information see the Introduction.

BLESSING

May God bless our dreams for justice and righteousness and fill us with courage to keep them alive. Amen

Blessing for Valentine's Day

PREPARATION   Valentine's Day is named after two 3rd century martyrs both named St. Valentine.
This blessing celebrates not only romantic love, but all deeply loving relationships, as well as the Source of all love.
Option 1 is intended to be used when you can be with your spouse, partner, friend or loved one(s).
Use option 2 if you are alone. Have paper and pen available. Gather together some pictures of your loved one(s).
Light a candle* and place a small candle for each person beside it.

WELCOME
For everything there is a season,
and a time for every matter under heaven.
Welcome to this time for reflection on God's love
that flows through us to others.

PRAYER
**Lover of all, you have shown us how to love each other
through your Son, Jesus. Thank you for your gift of love.
Let your love so fill our hearts that it spills over into all
our relationships. Amen**

BIBLE TEXT
Beloved, let us love one another, because love is from God;
everyone who loves is born of God and knows God.
Beloved, since God loved us so much, we also ought to love
one another. 1 John 4:7,11

REFLECTION
OPTION 1 — Hold hands and share with your loved one(s)
what you most love about the other. These sentence starters
might be helpful: **The things I most admire about you are . . .
I am grateful to you for . . . When I look at you,
I see/feel/think** . . . Then share how God has blessed your life
through this love.

OPTION 2 — Reflect on these same sentence starters and
then write a letter to your loved one(s), living or dead.

RITUAL ACTION
OPTION 1 — Take turns lighting a small candle from the
center candle, saying, **Because God loves me, I am able to
love you.**

OPTION 2 — Light a small candle for all those persons
in your life whom you love or have loved deeply.
As you light each candle, thank God for the gift of love.

*For more information see the Introduction.

BLESSING
May God continue to pour love into us, so that we might grow in our love for one another. Amen

Blessing for Mother's Day and Father's Day

PREPARATION For the purposes of this blessing, the term "mother" refers to the person(s) who mothered you and "father" to the person(s) who fathered you. Option 1 is for times when you are with the person(s). Set an empty blessing cup* on the table. Option 2 is for those times when they are not with you. In that case, place pictures of your mother/father on the table along with pencils/pens and a small piece of paper for everyone.

WELCOME

For everything there is a season,
and a time for every matter under heaven.
Welcome to this time of joyfully celebrating those people in our lives who have been God's parenting hands for us on earth.

PRAYER

Father and Mother God, from the beginning of time you have set aside mothers/fathers to give life, comfort, encouragement and guidance to their children. Today we remember the sometimes difficult, sometimes joyous task of motherhood/fatherhood and the blessings we have received from our mothers/fathers. Amen

BIBLE TEXT

"Honor your father and mother" — This is the first commandment with a promise: "so that it may be well with you and you may live long on the earth." Ephesians 6:2-3

REFLECTION

Take a moment to quietly reflect on your mother(s)/father(s). Then write down a single word or short phrase that best describes what your mother(s)/father(s) mean(s) to you. If you do this blessing year after year, focus on those particular attributes most obvious in the past year. These sentence starters may be helpful:
What I like best about you is . . .
What I am most thankful for is . . .

Then write a blessing for your mother(s)/father(s) beginning with these words: **Mother/Father, my prayer for you is . . .**

RITUAL ACTION

OPTION 1 — Place all pieces of paper in the blessing cup. Then present the blessing cup filled with personal blessings to your mother(s)/father(s) while repeating these words:
Thank you mother/father for your presence in my/our world. Your love has given me/us life.

OPTION 2 — Place the blessings in a card and mail them. If a parent is no longer living, send the blessings as a prayer.

*For more information see the Introduction.

BLESSING

May the love of God shine through all mothers/fathers. May all children find peace and hope in that love. Amen

Blessing for Memorial Day

PREPARATION Memorial Day was first observed in 1868 to decorate the graves of American Civil War dead and is now a national day to honor those members of the armed services killed during wartime. Many families use this day to honor anyone who has died in their family. Set out pictures of loved ones whom you want to remember on this day, particularly those who, in one way or another, have sacrificed their lives so that your life might be better. Place a candle* in the center of the pictures and a number of small candles around the pictures. Light the center candle.

WELCOME
For everything there is a season,
and a time for every matter under heaven.
Welcome to this time for remembering.

PRAYER
Dear God of our fathers and mothers, our forefathers and foremothers, give us an understanding mind and a grateful heart as we consider all who have sacrificed so that we might live. Amen

BIBLE TEXT
Truly I tell you, wherever this good news is proclaimed in the whole world, what she has done will be told in remembrance of her. Matthew 26:13

REFLECTION
Name each of the family members
or groups of people who have died and because of
whose life and death your life is different (ancestors,
those who have fought in wars, for civil rights,
for public safety, for better health care,
for better education . . .). Share or write in a journal* about
the sacrifices these people made.

These sentence starters may be helpful:

When I think about these people,
I am most grateful for . . .
I am most sad about . . .

RITUAL ACTION
Light a candle naming each person or group, allowing a moment of silence after each name.

SONG
Sing or say,
To God, with joy, our thanks we bring,
rememb'ring those today,
Who gave their lives, a sacrifice,
preserving freedom's way.   (Tune *Amazing Grace*)

*For more information see the Introduction.

BLESSING
May God, who journeyed with those before us, go with us this day, making our lives a blessing to all who come after us. Amen

Blessing for the Fourth of July

PREPARATION Independence Day was first observed in Philadelphia on July 8, 1776, at which time the Declaration of Independence was read aloud. In 1941, July 4th was set as a national holiday to celebrate freedom. Set out an American flag. Fill a blessing cup* and set it next to the flag.

WELCOME

For everything there is a season,
and a time for every matter under heaven.
Welcome to this time for celebrating our freedoms.

PRAYER

Dear God, you sent your Son to set us free from the oppression of sin and death. Help us treasure and preserve all other freedoms we have been given. Amen

BIBLE TEXT

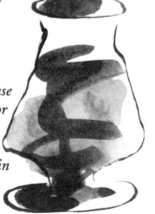

For you were called to freedom, brothers and sisters; only do not use your freedom as an opportunity for self-indulgence, but through love become servants to one another. For the whole law is summed up in a single commandment, "You shall love your neighbor as yourself." Galatians 5:13-14

REFLECTION

OPTION 1 — Name some freedoms you have that others do not experience.

OPTION 2 — Share or write in a journal,* finishing these sentences: **This year I am most grateful for: freedom from . . .** (oppression, hunger, fear . . .), **freedom to . . .** (worship, learn, work, care for others and for the earth . . .).

This year I am most concerned about helping others experience: freedom from . . . (oppression, hunger, fear . . .), **freedom to . . .** (worship, learn, work, care for others and for the earth . . .).

RITUAL ACTION

Hold the blessing cup and say, **This year I dedicate myself to work on preserving or helping others experience these freedoms: . . .** Drink from the blessing cup, and pass it on.

SONG OPTIONS

This Land is Your Land, America the Beautiful, God Bless America, My Country `tis of Thee, Lift Ev'ry Voice and Sing.

*For more information see the Introduction.

BLESSING

May we treasure the freedoms we have been given, using them always as gifts for the common good. Amen

Blessing for Labor Day

PREPARATION Labor Day originated in 1882 to honor the working class. This blessing honors the wide variety of workers who contribute to our well-being. Set out various common household objects: a loaf of bread, some fruit, an article of clothing, a toy, a craft item, a book, a newspaper.
Set a candle* in the center and arrange small candles around it. Light the center candle.

WELCOME
For everything there is a season,
and a time for every matter under heaven.
Welcome to this time for celebrating the work
we and others do, work that enriches lives.

PRAYER
God of our labors, give us eyes to see the value of our own work and grateful hearts for laborers all over the world whose work makes our lives more abundant. Amen

BIBLE TEXT
Let the favor of the Lord our God be upon us,
and prosper for us the work of our hands —
O prosper the work of our hands! Psalm 90:17

REFLECTION
Pick one or two of the objects. Trace as nearly as you can, the number of people who have labored so you can use these objects. Then name others who labor to make life better — those who collect garbage, work on roads or buildings; those who provide a wide variety of services; those who work in education, medicine, management . . .

RITUAL ACTION
Name one or two people or groups whose work you particularly appreciate (the migrant workers who picked the fruit, the trucker who transported it, the grocer who stocked it . . .). Light a small candle in honor of each of those persons or groups. Then pray this prayer,

Dear God, Jesus came that all might have life and have it abundantly. Give us vision and courage to strive for a world where all who labor may have good working conditions, fair wages, and fulfillment in their work. Amen

SONG
Sing or say:
The farmer and the baker are in God's hands,
The builder and the tailor are in God's hands,
The miner and the cleaner are in God's hands,
All who labor are in God's hands.
(Change the names to make your own verses.)
(Tune: *He's Got the Whole World in His Hands.*)

*For more information see the Introduction.

13

BLESSING
May our work and the work of others around the globe be a blessing to all. Amen

Blessing for the New School Year

PREPARATION This blessing is for the night prior to the beginning of the school year.
Have your child gather his or her backpack, book bag, or other supplies and place them on the floor in the center of the room.
In addition, if you have some small Christian symbol (a cross or picture) that will fit in the backpack, have that ready.
Also set out a bowl of water for making the sign of the cross.* Gather as a family around the school supplies. If you have more
than one child beginning a new school year, repeat the prayer, the text, the ritual action and the final blessing for each child.

WELCOME

For everything there is a season,
and a time for every matter under heaven.
Welcome to this time of change, excitement
and new opportunities.

PRAYER

Gracious God, you have promised
to keep us safe and holy. Be present with
(name) during this time of preparation
for school tomorrow. Give (name) an open
and eager mind. Protect all your children
from temptation, and guide them with
your love. Amen

BIBLE TEXT

(Name), the Lord will keep your going out
and your coming in from this time on and forevermore.
Psalm 121:8

REFLECTION

Invite those gathered (both parents and children) to share their
thoughts and feelings about the new school year by finishing
these sentences:
I'm scared about . . .
I'm worried about . . .
I'm excited about . . .

RITUAL ACTION

Parents and/or others not beginning school, make the sign
of the cross on the forehead of the child going to school while
saying these words, **(Name), Jesus is with you wherever you go.**

Then have the child going to school place the Christian
symbol in the backpack or book bag as an ongoing reminder
that Jesus is always present.

SONG

Sing or say, *As You Go on Your Way,* (p. 84).
(This song and the following blessing can also be done the
next day just as your child is preparing to leave for school.
Place your hand on his or her head as you say the blessing.)

*For more information see the Introduction.

BLESSING

(Name), may the love of Jesus be with you on your first day of school and throughout the year. I/we love you. Amen

Blessing for Halloween Eve of All Saints' Day

PREPARATION The name "Halloween" comes from the Christian celebration once called "Hallowmas," or "Allhallows," and now called "All Saints' Day." "Hallow" means "holy." Option 1 is to be done with children. You will need a pumpkin, a carving utensil, and a candle.* Option 2 is for adults. You will need a large candle* and many small candles.

WELCOME
For everything there is a season,
and a time for every matter under heaven.
Welcome to this time of remembering those, both living and dead, who have guided us on our spiritual journeys.

PRAYER
Dear God, on the eve of the festival of All Saints' Day, may we be reminded of those who have touched our lives with your grace and truth, bringing light and hope into our darkened places. May this Halloween be for us a hallowed experience. Amen

BIBLE TEXT
Therefore, since we are surrounded by so great a cloud of witnesses, let us also lay aside every weight and the sin that clings so closely, and let us run with perseverance the race that is set before us, looking to Jesus the pioneer and perfecter of our faith.
Hebrews 12:1-2a

REFLECTION
OPTION 1 — Ask the children to name people who have loved them and taught them the most about Jesus' love. Have each child say,
Thank you, saint (name), for teaching me about Jesus.

OPTION 2 — Share or write in a journal* about the people who have loved you and taught you the most about God's love. Who is in the 'cloud of witnesses' that surrounds your life right now? How are these people helping you to 'run with perseverance'?

15

RITUAL ACTION
OPTION 1 — Choose a Christian symbol (cross, fish, star, candle, lamb . . .) or a symbol for the person you have named as a saint. Clean out the pumpkin and carve that symbol into the shell. Put the candle into the pumpkin and light it.

OPTION 2 — Light a small candle in honor of each of the persons in your cloud of witnesses. Name them as their flame glows bright.

*For more information see the Introduction.

BLESSING

May the holiness of this night enter into us, the vision of the saints guide us, and the light of God forever shine through us.
Amen

Blessing for Thanksgiving Day

PREPARATION In 1863 President Abraham Lincoln appointed a national day of Thanksgiving. This celebration grew out of a long tradition of harvest festivals in many cultures and dated back in the United States to the colonial period. Canadian Thanksgiving is in October. Do this blessing while at the table before or after Thanksgiving dinner, or find a quiet time and space sometime during the day. Fill a blessing cup.*

WELCOME

For everything there is a season,
and a time for every matter under heaven.
Welcome to this time of hope-filled gratitude and honoring of the earth.

PRAYER

Maker of earth and sky, we praise you for the millions of creatures and living things you have made, for earth, air, fire and water that give us life. Give us grateful hearts for all your gifts and passionate commitment to the earth you have put in our care. Amen

BIBLE TEXT

You have given us dominion over the works of your hands; you have put all things under our feet. Psalm 8: 6

I will praise the name of God with a song; I will magnify God with thanksgiving! Psalm 69:30

REFLECTION

Share or write in a journal* about the things you are most thankful for in your life. Using these sentence starters may be helpful:
When I think about this country, I am most thankful for . . .
When I think about my family, I am most thankful for . . .
When I think about my life, I am most thankful for . . .
When I think about the earth, I am most thankful for . . .

God has given us many blessings and has also given human beings dominion over the earth. That means we have responsibility to care for and not waste what God has made. Share or write in a journal about ways you can show that responsibility in concrete action toward all parts of creation — the water, the land, the animals, the plants . . .

RITUAL ACTION

Pass the blessing cup, saying,
Thank you, God, for life and for all creation.
Make us trustworthy care-takers of all you have made. Amen

*For more information see the Introduction.

BLESSING

May the enduring love of our Creator fill us with gratitude and responsibility for all we have been given. Amen

Blessing for Heritage Holidays

PREPARATION As a part of their heritage, many people have special holidays of ethnic origin that can be celebrated. Prepare special foods. Set out artifacts or other symbols to indicate the background of this holiday. Fill a blessing cup.*

WELCOME
For everything there is a season,
and a time for every matter under heaven.
Welcome to this celebration of _____.

PRAYER
O God of history and of peoples all over the world, we thank you for all that makes us who we are--for our ancestors, for our families, for those who come after us, for the richness of tradition we have been given. Help us hold as precious all that gives our life meaning. Amen

BIBLE TEXT
Let the peoples praise you, O God;
let all the peoples praise you. Let the
nations be glad and sing for joy . . .
Psalm 67:3-4a

Come and see what the Lord has done. God has done
awesome deeds among mortals. Psalm 66:5

REFLECTION
Each generation needs to learn anew its family's ethnic history. Ask the oldest members of the family to share their cultural/familial stories and wisdom. Prompt children to ask the following questions:
Why do we celebrate this day?
What is the history of this day?
In what ways can we see God at work in this event
and in the memory of this event?

RITUAL ACTION
Pass the blessing cup, saying,
We praise you, God, for the
awesome deeds you have done.

SONG
Learn and sing songs from your heritage, particularly songs you can sing in another language. Incorporate folk dances and costumes, if possible.

*For more information see the Introduction.

BLESSING
May the God of history bless our remembrance of this day and our memory of the heritage from which we have descended.
Amen

Blessing for the Changing of the Seasons

PREPARATION This blessing is to be celebrated on or near the solstices (December and June) and equinoxes (March and September) or at the first sign of the changing seasons. Hold the blessing outside, if possible. Find symbols that represent the current season and the coming season (bare branches, seeds, flowers, changing leaves . . .). Arrange symbols from the current season on a table or on the ground, and set symbols for the coming season aside.

WELCOME

For everything there is a season,
and a time for every matter under heaven.
Welcome to the changing of the seasons.

PRAYER

Holy One, Mother of Creation, Father of Life, bless our gathering, that we may honor the rhythms of the earth as witnesses to your extravagant love and faithfulness. Amen

BIBLE TEXT

As long as the earth endures, seedtime and harvest, cold and heat, summer and winter, day and night, shall not cease.
Genesis 8:22

REFLECTION

Share or write in a journal* about the following questions:
How have I seen the presence of God revealed this past season in my life? In nature?

PRAYER

Thank you, God of cycles and rhythms, for making yourself known to us in the seasons of the earth and the seasons of our lives. Amen

RITUAL ACTION

Remove old symbols and replace them with the new.

REFLECTION

Share or write in a journal* about the following question:
What do I hope for as I enter this new season?
Name one thing from nature that will be your special reminder of God's presence in the coming season.

PRAYER

God of rhythms and cycles, open our hearts and all our senses to your presence in nature during the coming season. Amen

If possible, take a walk in your neighborhood, a park or a natural area. Pay special attention to the sights, sounds, smells, and texture of the natural world. What does nature teach us about God?

*For more information see the Introduction.

BLESSING

May we trust that this season, like all others, will bear witness to God's extravagant love and faithfulness. Amen

SEASONS OF OUR LIVES

Blessing Our Developmental Milestones

PREPARATION Developmental milestones are all of those firsts in life, those significant or insignificant moments that mark change and growth toward maturity. In some cases, these milestones will be celebrated by parents or other adults for the milestone of a child (a child's first step, a first tooth . . .). At other times, the person reaching a milestone will be a part of, or even leading, the celebration (learning the alphabet, learning to ride a bike, learning how to use a computer . . .). In both instances, set aside a special time and fill a blessing cup.*

WELCOME
For everything there is a season,
and a time for every matter under heaven.
Welcome to this time of marking
and celebrating growth and change.

PRAYER
Dearest Jesus, you were once a small child who grew and developed and changed. Be with us now as we celebrate this special moment. Always help us remember that you will be with us throughout life, making each stage of life a blessing. Amen

TEXT
The child grew, and was weaned; and Abraham made a great feast on the day that Isaac was weaned.
Genesis 21:8

The child [Jesus] grew and became strong, filled with wisdom, and the favor of God was upon him.
Luke 2:40

REFLECTION
Developmental milestones mark the transition from one stage of life into another. With every transition something is lost and something is gained, something ends and something begins. Reflect on the milestone that has just occurred to you or your child. Share with those gathered or write in a journal.* You may want to use the following sentence starters:

This milestone marks the end of . . .
This milestone marks the beginning of . . .
This milestone makes me feel . . .

If the person experiencing this milestone is a child who is old enough to communicate, ask him or her to fill in the blank and finish this sentence:
I am _____ (excited, scared, nervous, happy, sad . . .)
about this new stage of life, because . . .

RITUAL ACTION
Pass the blessing cup, saying, **Blessings to you, (name),**
as you grow and change.

*For more information see the Introduction.

BLESSING
May God bless this milestone and help us treasure every new stage of life. Amen

Blessing Our Adolescent Body Changes

PREPARATION Adolescent body changes take place over a number of years and are often difficult to discuss. This blessing can help you in your conversation about these changes. Fill a blessing cup* with the adolescent's favorite juice and place it on a table, surrounded by pictures of the adolescent and other family members from birth to the age of the adolescent. You may also wish to give a special gift to the adolescent and/or take a picture to remember the celebration. This blessing may be expanded and modified specifically for boys or girls.

WELCOME
*For everything there is a season,
and a time for every matter under heaven.*
Welcome to this time for celebrating
our changing bodies.

PRAYER
**Creator God, the Bible
tells us our bodies are
temples of your Holy Spirit.
Bless (name) as her/his body
is changing and growing. Amen**

BIBLE TEXT
*And the man and his wife were
both naked, and were not ashamed . . .
So when the woman saw . . . that the tree was to be desired to
make one wise, she took of its fruit and ate; and she also gave
some to her husband, who was with her, and he ate.*

*Then the eyes of both were opened, and they knew that
they were naked; and they sewed fig leaves together and
made loincloths for themselves.*
Genesis 2:25, 3:6-7

REFLECTION
This story about the first male and female also describes what it is like to grow up. As young children, we are not embarrassed to be naked. But, as we grow up, our bodies change, and we may become more self-conscious in front of other people. (That is why Adam and Eve made clothes for themselves.) We also become curious about lots of things we did not care about before (like Adam and Eve wanting to be wise).

Have those gathered recall and share joyful childhood memories of (name). Then share feelings about (name) growing up. Finishing these sentences may be helpful: **I'm excited about . . . I'm curious about . . . I'm nervous about . . .** Encourage the adolescent to share as much or as little as she or he likes.

RITUAL ACTION
Gather around the adolescent, placing your hands on his or her head, and say these words from Psalm 139:14.
We praise you, God, for (name) is fearfully and wonderfully made. Wonderful are your works; that we know very well.
Then pass the blessing cup, saying,
Welcome to this new stage of life.

*For more information see the Introduction.

BLESSING
May God, who knit you together and who dwells within you, bless your changing body. Amen

Blessing upon Getting a Driver's License

PREPARATION In our culture, getting a driver's license, particularly for a teenager, is a rite of passage that should be honored. It marks a major leap in the independence and responsibility of a teenager. Set a time when there will be no distractions and the parents/guardians and the teenager can do the blessing together.
Set out the driver's license, car keys, paper and pencil/pen. Fill a blessing cup.*

WELCOME

For everything there is a season,
and a time for every matter under heaven.
Welcome to this time of celebrating growing independence and increased responsibility.

PRAYER

Guardian of all, thank you for bringing us to this moment when (name) has received a driver's license. Watch over and protect all drivers. Grant wisdom and maturity to (name) and fill us all with trust in your guiding hand. Amen

BIBLE TEXT

How can young people keep their way pure? By guarding it according to your word. With my whole heart I seek you; do not let me stray from your commandments. Psalm 119:9-10

REFLECTION

A driver's license is a powerful thing. It gives people opportunities for independence and places upon them enormous responsibility. Take turns finishing these sentences:
This driver's license is a good thing because . . .
Problems that could arise because of this license are . . .

RITUAL ACTION

Talk through and write down a covenant between parent(s) and teenager in which expectations are agreed upon. For instance, where will the teenager have permission to drive? What is expected from the new driver (obeying traffic rules, running errands on occasion, not overloading the car with friends, coming home on time. . .)?

What is expected from the parent(s) (trust unless that trust is broken. . .)? Determine who is expected to pay for gas, insurance and repairs. When you have written out a covenant that all parties agree to, sign it.

Then pass the blessing cup, saying a blessing of your own, or, (Name), I celebrate your **new independence and responsibility.**

*For more information see the Introduction.

BLESSING

May God bless this new driver and keep us all safe. Amen

Blessing Our Graduations and Achievements

PREPARATION Use this blessing at a graduation party or any gathering honoring an achievement, large or small (job promotion, school or sports achievement, recital, award . . .). Fill glasses for everyone for making a toast. If you are celebrating alone, adapt as best fits your accomplishment.

WELCOME
For everything there is a season,
and a time for every matter under heaven.
Welcome to this celebration of (name)'s achievement of . . .

PRAYER
Loving God, we thank you for times in our lives when we can celebrate our accomplishments. Thank you for the gifts and abilities you have given (name) that enabled this achievement, one that would not have been possible had it not been for you. With gratefulness, we acknowledge your presence and guidance in our lives. In Jesus' name we pray. Amen

BIBLE TEXT
Finally, beloved, whatever is true, whatever is honorable, whatever is just, whatever is pure, whatever is pleasing, whatever is commendable, if there is any excellence and if there is anything worthy of praise, think about these things.

Keep on doing the things that you have learned and received and heard and seen in me, and the God of peace will be with you. Philippians 4:8-9

REFLECTION
Have the one honored share thoughts about the following: **What makes this achievement special for you? What, if any, were the greatest obstacles you had to overcome? What gifts did God give you that allowed you to achieve this goal? Who are the people you need to thank for their support and help?**

Then have those doing the honoring express their words of congratulations!

RITUAL ACTION
Raise your glasses in honor of the achievement, saying, **Well done! May the God of peace continue to bless you!**

BLESSING
May God bless us all with a humble spirit, a grateful heart, a dedicated mind, and willing hands of service as we pursue what is commendable in God's eyes. Amen

Blessing for Those Leaving Home

PREPARATION This blessing is intended to be used when children become young adults and move out of the family home heading for college, the military, jobs . . . Life changes dramatically for the person leaving, but also for those remaining at home. This blessing gives all present a chance to express their thoughts and feelings about this change. Set a begging bowl* on a table.

WELCOME
For everything there is a season,
and a time for every matter under heaven.
Welcome to this time of saying good-bye as one member leaves the family nest.

PRAYER
Thank you, God,
for the years of
learning and growing, of
loving and giving, we have
had together. We ask your
grace upon (name) who is leaving and
on those who remain behind. Give us all we need as we move into a new stage of life, separated by space, but bound together in love. Amen

BIBLE TEXT
Where can I go from your spirit? Or where can I flee from your presence? . . . If I take the wings of the morning and settle at the farthest limits of the sea, even there your hand shall lead me, and your right hand shall hold me fast.
Psalm 139:7, 9-10

REFLECTION
The image of God's hand leading us wherever we go, whether together or apart, is a comforting one. Have all present finish these sentences:

When I look ahead, I feel saddest about . . .
I feel most excited about . . .
My prayer for the future is . . .
During the days and weeks ahead, what I need from you who love me is . . .

RITUAL ACTION
Pass the begging bowl from person to person, asking each person to hold it up and say, **Ever-present God, please lead me and give me all I need in the days ahead.**

SONG
Place your hands on the person leaving and sing or say, *As You Go on Your Way,* (p. 84).

*For more information see the Introduction.

BLESSING
May the hand of God hold us fast, keeping us safe from all danger. Amen

Blessing for Those Traveling

PREPARATION This blessing can be initiated by those remaining behind, as a way of sending off loved ones, or by those traveling. Place a bowl of water on a table for making the sign of the cross.*

WELCOME

For everything there is a season,
and a time for every matter under heaven.
We pause to ask for God's presence to be with (name) during this journey.

PRAYER

Good and gracious God, as this journey is about to begin, help me/us to trust that you have good things in store. Watch over all who travel. Make us ever mindful of your presence. Amen

BIBLE TEXT

It is the Lord who goes before you. God will be with you; God will not fail you or forsake you. Do not fear or be dismayed.
Deuteronomy 31:8

REFLECTION

As the Bible says, God will be with you wherever you go. Reflect on the nature of your journey: **Where are you going? Why are you going there? How long will you be there?** Think about, write in a journal* about or share: **What is it about this journey that you anticipate with apprehension? What is it about this journey that you anticipate with joy?**

RITUAL ACTION

Make the sign of the cross on your own forehead, if you are alone, or on the foreheads of all who are traveling. If some are traveling and others are remaining behind, have those remaining make the sign of the cross on the forehead(s) of the traveler(s), saying,
Remember, God goes with you.

In some families, one spouse/parent travels often on work related matters and can easily lose touch with the family. Consider these ritual actions:
Every night both those traveling and those at home write in a journal about their highs and lows of the day, a journal that can be shared when the traveler returns. Or, draw a picture of some special part of the day. Sharing these memories can be an important part of welcoming the traveler home.

SONG

Sing or say, *As You Go on Your Way,* (p. 84).
(Use the appropriate variation.)

*For more information see the Introduction.

BLESSING

May we always remember that God goes with us wherever we go. Amen

Blessing for New Beginnings

PREPARATION Have everyone gathered who is involved in this new beginning write the name of the new beginning (the place to which you are moving, the job you are taking . . .) at the top of a piece of paper.
Set out a picture of Jesus, a cross, or a Bible, and a candle.* Light the candle.

WELCOME
For everything there is a season,
and a time for every matter under heaven.
Welcome to a time for blessing this start of something new.

PRAYER
Dear Lord, give to (name) direction during this time, clear focus on the possibilities for this new beginning, help in the many preparations, and trust that all will be well. Amen

BIBLE TEXT
Do not worry about anything, but in everything by prayer and supplication with thanksgiving let your requests be made known to God. And the peace of God, which surpasses all understanding, will guard your hearts and your minds in Christ Jesus. Philippians 4:6-7

REFLECTION
On your paper under the title of the new beginning, complete the following sentences:
I hope that . . .
I worry about . . .
I will be disappointed if . . .
I am excited about . . . Share your responses.

RITUAL ACTION
OPTION 1 — Each person in turns holds his or her paper up and says, **I give all hopes and worries to God who wants only what is best for me.** Place the paper on the table next to the picture or cross or in the Bible.

OPTION 2 — Spend time deep breathing.* Breathe in your hopes and God's peace and love, and breathe out your fears, expectations, and worries.

Place your paper next to the picture or cross or in the Bible, letting go of your worries and entrusting your hopes to God. Keep this list with you during the days and weeks ahead. As worries or fears arise, remember you have offered them all to Jesus.

*For more information see the Introduction.

BLESSING
May we feel peace, trusting that God will be present in all new beginnings, carrying our hopes and bringing us life. Amen

Blessing for a New Home

PREPARATION Invite family and friends to your new home. Place a small candle in each room to be blessed and carry a lit candle with you. Mark the following verses in your Bible for easy reference: Proverbs 24:3; Psalm 121:8; John 13:34; Psalm 145:15-16; Psalm 4:8; Isaiah 32:18. Add hymns or songs if you like. If you are leading this blessing in someone else's house, change pronouns when necessary.

WELCOME
For everything there is a season,
and a time for every matter under heaven.
Welcome to this time for blessing our home.

RITUAL ACTION
(Gather outside, if possible.) Read Proverbs 24:3.
Let us pray: **O God, as candles bring light to this home, so enable (home owners) to be your light in this neighborhood. In Jesus' name we pray. Amen**
Light the candle and say, **Christ is present!**
(Move to the entrance.)

Read Psalm 121:8. **Let us pray: Defender God, protect and guide those of us who live here; our going out and our coming in; and let us share the hospitality of this home with all who visit, that those who enter may know your love and peace. Amen**
Light the candle and say, **Christ is present!**
(Move to the family or living room.)

Read John 13:34. **Let us pray: Giver of joy and love, bless all who share this room that through you we may be bound together in a community of love. Amen**
Light the candle and say, **Christ is present!**
(Move to the kitchen/dining room.)

Read Psalm 145:15-16. **Let us pray: Blessed are you, Lord of heaven and earth, for you give us food and drink to sustain our lives and make our hearts glad. Help us to be grateful for all your mercies and mindful of the needs of others. Amen**
Light the candle and say, **Christ is present!**
(Move to the bedrooms.)

Read Psalm 4:8. **Let us pray: Lord, you provide rest for the weary and renewal for our bodies and spirits. Bless our times of rest that we might be refreshed and energized for your service. Amen**
Light the candle and say, **Christ is present!**
(Return to the family or living room.)

Read Isaiah 32:18. **Let us pray: O God, we pray you will bless this home and bless (names) with your gracious presence. Let your love be our inspiration, your wisdom our guide, your truth our light, and your peace our benediction, through Jesus Christ our Lord. Amen**

Join hands and pray the Lord's Prayer (p. 84).

BLESSING
May the Lord watch over us as we go out and come in now and forever. Amen

Blessing for the Single Life

PREPARATION This blessing can be done alone (option 1) or with other single people (option 2).
If alone, gather pictures or mementos of people, either alive or dead, who have positively touched your life.
Create a circle of small candles* and place them around the pictures and light them. If you are with friends, fill a blessing cup.*

WELCOME

For everything there is a season,
and a time for every matter under heaven.
Welcome to this time of growing contentment with
who I am and whose I am.

PRAYER

O Lord, you have granted me the gift of being single.
Help me to see that with you I am never alone. With you I can
be content with my situation and thrive in my life. Amen

BIBLE TEXT

. . . for I have learned to be content with whatever I have.
I know what it is to have little, and I know what it is to
have plenty. In any and all circumstances I have learned
the secret of being well-fed and of going hungry, of having
plenty and of being in need. I can do all things through
Christ who strengthens me.
Philippians 4:11-13

REFLECTION

OPTION 1 — Reflect or write in a journal*about the blessings
and difficulties of the single life. Then look at each of the
pictures on the table. Reflect or write about the relationships
you have developed with each of these people and with God.
Try to recall times in your life when they have not been
physically present, yet you have felt their presence.

OPTION 2 — Share with one another the blessings and
difficulties you have experienced in the single life.

RITUAL ACTION

OPTION 1 — Make the sign of the cross* and say,
I am a child of God and I can do all things through Christ
who strengthens me.

OPTION 2 — Pass the blessing cup, saying a blessing of
your own, or, **(Name), you can do all things through Christ
who strengthens you.**

*For more information see the Introduction.

BLESSING

May our lives be blessed with a loving community, given to us by God, enabling us to rejoice in all that is and all that will be.
Amen

Blessing for Times of Loss and/or Gratitude

PREPARATION Sometimes our hearts nearly burst with pure gratitude and joy. Sometimes loss washes over us and we feel as if we might drown in the sorrow. Often, however, these emotions are intermingled. We grieve the loss of property in a tornado, but are grateful for our lives being saved. We are angry over the theft of our precious belongings, but are grateful we weren't home. Adapt this blessing to meet your needs. Option 1 focuses on loss, option 2 on gratitude. Do one or both of the options. Fill a blessing cup.*

WELCOME
For everything there is a season,
and a time for every matter under heaven.
Welcome to this time for (grieving loss and/or giving thanks).

PRAYER
God of faith, hope, and love, this prayer rises before you from hearts filled with (loss and/or gratitude). Be present during this time. Give us all we need for the day.
In Jesus' name we pray. Amen

BIBLE TEXT
Rejoice always, pray without ceasing, give thanks in all circumstances; for this is the will of God in Christ Jesus for you. 1 Thessalonians 5: 16-18

REFLECTION
OPTION 1 — Share or write in a journal,* naming those things that have been lost:
tangible things (home, possessions . . .),
intangible qualities (trust, serenity . . .),
and beliefs (God will always protect me, people are generally good, this person is trustworthy . . .).

Then finish these sentences:

I am most angry about . . .
I am most sad about . . .
If only I had . . .

OPTION 2 — Share or write in a journal,* naming all you are grateful for.
Then finish these sentences:

I am grateful for _____ because . . .
Before this happened,
I was most worried about . . .
One thing I hope for now is . . .

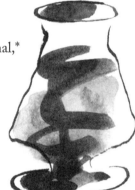

RITUAL ACTION
OPTION 1 — Pass the blessing cup, saying,
I trust in you, God, to see me through this loss.

OPTION 2 — Pass the blessing cup, saying,
Thank you, God, for . . .

*For more information see the Introduction.

BLESSING
May God's love fill our hearts with gratitude for our blessings and courage for the day. Amen

Blessing for a New Pet

PREPARATION Option 1 in this blessing is to be used with families with children. Option 2 is for adults. Have available paper, pencils/pens, and colors.

WELCOME
For everything there is a season,
and a time for every matter under heaven.
Welcome to this time of rejoicing and claiming responsibility for one of God's creatures.

PRAYER
Creator of all things, bless us as we take into our home one of your beloved creatures. Give us knowledgeable minds and compassionate hearts. Amen

BIBLE TEXT
God said, "This is the sign of the covenant that I make between me and you and every living creature that is with you, for all future generations: I have set my rainbow in the clouds, and it shall be a sign of the covenant between me and the earth." Genesis 9:12-13

REFLECTION
OPTION 1 — Gather around the kitchen table. Have the new pet nearby. Brainstorm a list of all the tasks and responsibilities involved in having this pet. Ask the children to volunteer for the tasks they want to do.

Write out a covenant for the care of the pet, which could take this form: **We, the (name) family, promise to care for (name of pet), who is one of God's loved creatures. To accomplish this, (name) will put out the food each day, (name) will take the pet outside, (name) will pay for veterinarian bills . . .**
Try to include everyone in the family with some responsibility both for the tasks and for taking time to enjoy this pet as God's gift to you.

OPTION 2 — Obtain and read information on the care of your particular pet. Work out a schedule so the pet will be taken care of and you will have time to enjoy this pet as God's gift to you.

RITUAL ACTION
Draw or find a picture of a rainbow. God uses the rainbow as a sign of promise to Noah and to every living creature on the ark that God will never again allow the earth to be destroyed by a flood. Put your rainbow picture in some obvious place so you will always be reminded of your covenant to love and responsibly care for your pet.

Hold or touch the pet, saying,
God bless you, (name). Welcome to the family.

BLESSING
May the God of all creation and all creatures bless the addition of this pet to this home. Amen

Blessing for the Death of a Pet

PREPARATION The death of a pet affects people in a variety of ways. Sometimes it is merely a time of instruction for children on the rhythms of life (for instance, when a goldfish dies). Other times it feels like, and in fact is, the death of a beloved member of the family. Adjust this blessing to meet your needs. Also, your ritual action will depend in part on the laws of your community for the disposal of the animal remains.

WELCOME
For everything there is a season,
and a time for every matter under heaven.
Welcome to this time for sharing our
sadness and saying good-bye to (name).

PRAYER
Creator God, you made (name) and all creatures,
large and small. Thank you for (name) and for all the ways
(name) blessed me/us. Be here now, as I/we say good-bye and
give (name) back to you. Amen

BIBLE TEXT
And God said, "Let the earth bring forth living creatures
of every kind . . ." And it was so. God made the wild animals
of the earth of every kind, and the cattle of every kind,
and everything that creeps upon the ground of every kind.
And God saw that it was good. Genesis 1:24-25.

REFLECTION
Share all your fondest memories of your pet or write in a journal,* perhaps writing a letter to your pet. Talk or write about what will be different in your life now. Allow yourself and others to grieve this loss openly and for as long as is necessary. If you have children who are concerned about where their pet is now, assure them that God loves all God's creatures.

RITUAL ACTION
If you are allowed to bury pets on your property, dig a grave for your pet, wrap it in a special blanket and bury it. If your pet must be cremated, bring the ashes home and mix them with dirt in the ground or in a planter. As you bury your pet or mix its ashes into the ground, say these words, **Good-bye, (name).** **Thank you for being with me/us. Now I/we give you back to your Creator.**

Then, plant something that will bloom or bear fruit as a yearly reminder of the joy and nourishment your pet brought to your life.

*For more information see the Introduction.

BLESSING
May the God of creation be with us in our sadness and comfort our spirits. Amen

Blessing of Encouragement for Care-Givers

PREPARATION Many people find themselves in the position of being the primary care-giver for someone: a spouse caring for a disabled spouse, adult children caring for aging parents or other relatives, grandparents caring for grandchildren, parents caring for small children or a child with special needs, for example. This blessing is for care-givers who are feeling under-appreciated, burdened and weary. It can be initiated by the care-giver or a friend in support of the care-giver. Set out a small bowl of oil or water for making the sign of the cross.* Light candles* representing Christ's presence with you.

WELCOME
For everything there is a season,
and a time for every matter under heaven.
Welcome to this time of rest and renewal.

PRAYER
Jesus, you showed compassion to your apostles, taking them away to rest. Show now your compassion for (name of care-giver) by providing assurance of your care, strength for the day, and trust in your mercy. Amen

BIBLE TEXT
The apostles gathered around Jesus, and told him all that they had done and taught. He said to them, "Come away to a deserted place all by yourselves and rest a while." For many were coming and going, and they had no leisure even to eat.
Mark 6:30-32

REFLECTION
The text tells us that people with needs pressed in on Jesus and his apostles. They felt exhausted and needed time for rest and renewal. Share or write in a journal* how you feel when the needs of others press in on you.

These sentence starters might be helpful:

Even though I love the person I am caring for, sometimes I feel . . . (resentful, angry, without hope . . .). My physical reactions to meeting the constant needs of another are . . . (exhaustion, muscle soreness, back aches . . .).

Share or write in a journal about ways you can follow Jesus' example and get away and rest (for instance, asking other professionals or volunteer care-givers for help; reaching out for help in releasing resentments, angers; believing that while we give the care, God gives the cure — we can let go).
Go through the list and pick out one or two actions.
Finish this sentence:
Today I will follow Jesus' lead and take care of myself by . . .

RITUAL ACTION
Make the sign of the cross on the care-giver's forehead, saying, **(Name), you are a loved co-worker with God, precious and worthy of rest.** Then pray, **God, give (name) trust in your loving care for all. Let (name) rest secure in the hollow of your hand. Amen**

*For more information see the Introduction.

BLESSING
May all be restored and renewed by Jesus' example and God's promise of love. Amen

Blessing for an Ill Friend or Family Member

PREPARATION This blessing can be done either alone or with the ill person.
Set out a bowl of water or oil for making the sign of the cross,* and, if permitted, a candle* representing Christ's healing light.
If desired set out a cross, picture, or image of Jesus, bringing to mind Jesus' ministry of healing. Light the candle.

WELCOME
For everything there is a season,
and a time for every matter under heaven.
Welcome to this time of prayer and hope.

PRAYER
Christ, our Healer, grant that (name of ill person)
will feel your Spirit and healing presence today as
he/she struggles with (illness). Amen

BIBLE TEXT
As the sun was setting, all those who had any who
were sick with various kinds of diseases brought
them to Jesus; and he laid his hands on them and
cured them. Luke 4:40

"Come to me, all you that are weary and are
carrying heavy burdens, and I will give you rest."
Matthew 11:28

REFLECTION
(If the illness is not life-threatening or serious, go directly
to the ritual action.) Think about times when the ill person
was healthy. Share or write in a journal* your memories and
feelings about those times and also your fears about the future,
fears caused by the illness.

RITUAL ACTION
OPTION 1 — Pray this prayer or a prayer of your own.
(If you are with the ill person, lay your hands on the person
while praying.) **Dear Lord, grant healing of body, mind,**
and spirit to (name). Give me/us patience in waiting and
confidence in your loving care. Amen
Then make the sign of the cross on your forehead and,
if possible, the forehead of the ill person, saying,
You belong to Christ.
Pray the Lord's Prayer (p. 84).

OPTION 2 — Close your eyes and do some deep breathing.*
Visualize* the healing light of Christ moving through the ill
person. Pray the prayer in option 1 or one of your own. (If you
are with the ill person, lay your hands on the person while
praying.) Then make the sign of the cross on your
forehead and the forehead of the ill person, if possible, saying,
I claim the healing power of Jesus for you.
Pray the Lord's Prayer (p. 84).

*For more information see the Introduction.

BLESSING
May we find rest and healing in the presence of Christ. Amen

Blessing before Surgery

PREPARATION This blessing can either be done by a friend or family member for the person having the surgery (option 1) or by the person having the surgery (option 2). Light a candle,* if permitted, representing Christ's light. Set out a bowl of oil or water for making the sign of the cross.*

WELCOME
For everything there is a season,
and a time for every matter under heaven.
Welcome to this time of hope for health and newness.

PRAYER
O Christ, our light and life, may this surgery bring healing to (name) in every way possible. May the doctors and nurses who care for (name) be filled with wisdom and compassion. Steady their hands and minds and guide their actions. Amen

BIBLE TEXT
When I am afraid, I put my trust in you . . . in God I trust
without a fear. What can flesh do to me?
Psalm 56:3-4

REFLECTION
As we face surgery of any kind, often fears accompany us. In what way has your life or the life of the person you love been held back due to the illness or injury? What if your desired outcome does not happen? What are some possibilities for life after successful surgery? Share with those present or write in a journal.*

RITUAL ACTION
OPTION 1 — Lay your hands on the head or body of the person facing surgery and pray, **In the name of Jesus, I lay my hands on you, praying that God will bring you strength and peace, and that you might know the healing power of Christ's presence. Amen**
Make the sign of the cross on his or her forehead, saying, **You are held in God's hands.**

OPTION 2 — Make the sign of the cross on your forehead, saying, **I place myself in God's loving hands.**

OPTION 3 — Focus on the lit candle and visualize* yourself or your loved one in surgery. See the doctors and nurses caring gently and competently for you or your loved one. Now imagine the room surrounded by the light of Christ, and see Christ's light infusing every part of the surgery, every person involved, every instrument used. Imagine the light wrapped around you or your loved one. Hold that image for a few moments. Now see yourself or your loved one healed. Pray a prayer of your own or, **Jesus Christ, thank you for holding (name) in your healing arms. Amen**

*For more information see the Introduction.

BLESSING
May Christ's healing light surround us and make us whole. Amen

Blessing for Those Struggling with Infertility

PREPARATION A couple's struggle with infertility is laced with the agonizing tension between hope and despair, acceptance and anger, and the rising and dying of life's dreams. This blessing can be done at any time, but particularly during those times when tests are being done, when hope for conception is high, or when the failure to conceive is weighing heavily. To prepare for this blessing, find a quiet time and space. Designate a candle that can be used as a hope candle along with two small candles for options 1 and 2. If you are alone, adapt this blessing accordingly.

WELCOME

For everything there is a season,
and a time for every matter under heaven.
Welcome to this time for expressing hope for conceiving a child and the fear of not being able to do so.

PRAYER

O God, Creator of all children, thank you for the yearning we have to parent a child. Give us open hearts and overflowing love for all children, knowing they are your treasures and joy. Amen

BIBLE TEXT

In the day of my trouble I seek the Lord; in the night my hand is stretched out without wearying; my soul refuses to be comforted. Psalm 77:2 *Let your steadfast love, O Lord, be upon us, even as we hope in you.* Psalm 33:22

REFLECTION AND RITUAL ACTION

OPTION 1 (for times of testing for infertility) — Share what makes you fearful and hopeful. Light the hope candle. Then each person lights a small candle, saying,

I claim my hope in Christ to calm my anxieties and fear. Then pray, **O God, hear our plea to conceive a child. Give us love for ourselves and each other, confidence in our doctors, patience with our bodies, and a spirit of peace. Amen**

OPTION 2 (for times of hope for conception) — Light the two small candles. Share your fears and hopes and what words of affirmation or encouragement you need from each other. Light the hope candle from the two small candles as a symbol of the mother and father joining together to create a new life. Then pray, **O God, we pray you would work your miracle of conception and develop a healthy baby in (name)'s womb. Give us patience in these anxious days of waiting and renewed hope for the blessing of a child. Amen**

OPTION 3 (for after finding out that conception has not happened) — Light the hope candle. Reread the Bible text. Share the ways your soul refuses to be comforted. Then pray this prayer, **O God, be with us in this time of disappointment and despair. Comfort us in our sorrow. Renew us. Give us vision for the life you want us to lead. Amen**

BLESSING

May the God of all creation fill us with patient hope that we will be blessed with a child to love and raise. Amen

Blessing for Times of Disappointment with Ourselves

PREPARATION Because we are human, we all go through times when we recognize we have made a mistake, blundered, held onto disappointments with others, sinned, or failed in some way. God can use such times as an opportunity to teach us something about God's forgiving love and our potential, or perhaps to direct us down a new path. This blessing can be done either alone or with trusted friends. Set out paper, pencil/pen and a begging bowl.*

WELCOME
For everything there is a season,
and a time for every matter under heaven.
Welcome to this blessing that acknowledges our
human frailty and claims God's patience and power.

PRAYER
**Gracious God, you are patient in our striving, loving in failure,
and encouraging always. Give me/us the grace to accept the
disappointments in life with resiliency and hope born in the
resurrection of Jesus, and nurtured in the new possibilities of
the Spirit. Amen**

BIBLE TEXT
*Not that I have already obtained this [the resurrection from
the dead] or have already reached the goal; but I press on to
make it my own, because Christ Jesus has made me his own.
Beloved, I do not consider that I have made it my own; but
this one thing I do: forgetting what lies behind and straining
forward to what lies ahead, I press on toward the goal for
the prize of the heavenly call of God in Christ Jesus.*
Philippians 3:12-14

REFLECTION
Share or write in a journal*about your situation, including
your feelings about the situation and yourself. The text
suggests, "forgetting what lies behind . . ." What is the most
difficult part of leaving this particular disappointment behind
you? The text also says, "straining forward . . ." What insights
have you gained about yourself, about others, and about Christ
that will help you move through this current disappointment
in yourself? It may be helpful to consider how you have
overcome such times in the past.

RITUAL ACTION
Hold the begging bowl, saying, **God, fill me with whatever
I can learn from this hard time and whatever I need to move
beyond it. Amen**

If others are present, as they gather around you and place their
hands on your head or shoulders, they may pray prayers of
their own or one may say, **(Name), Christ is walking with you
and so are we.**

*For more information see the Introduction.

BLESSING
**May our forgiving God bless us with forgiveness of ourselves and others, encouragement to meet the new day,
and confidence in God's presence in our lives. Amen**

Blessing for Times of Weariness and Muddling Through

PREPARATION Set a candle* in the center of an empty area. Light the candle. Sit in silence and spend a few moments looking at the light. If more than one person is doing this blessing, change pronouns accordingly.

WELCOME

For everything there is a season,
and a time for every matter under heaven.
Welcome to this time for resting and gaining strength.

PRAYER

Dear Jesus, remember me in my weariness, during times when hope has faded, when the future looks as bleak as the present, and the tasks of life drain away my joy. Pour your love and hope into me to give me strength to endure. Amen

BIBLE TEXT

I am worn out, O Lord; have pity on me! Give me strength; I am completely exhausted. Psalm 6:2 (TEV)

Cast all your anxieties on God, because God cares for you. I Peter 5:7.

We also boast in our sufferings, knowing that suffering produces endurance, and endurance produces character, and character produces hope, and hope does not disappoint us, because God's love has been poured into our hearts . . . Romans 5:3-5

REFLECTION

Finish this sentence in as many ways as you can:
If _____, then my life would be better.
For instance, If the baby started sleeping through the night . . .
If our teenager grew up . . . If my boss would let up on me . . .
If this pain would go away . . . If I didn't have to care for . . .

Go through your "If . . ." sentences and try to think of something you are grateful for in each situation, even as things are. Say a prayer of gratitude for each of these things. If there is nothing to be grateful for in the situation, pray it will end soon.

RITUAL ACTION

OPTION 1—Remembering Christ, who said,
Come to me all you who labor and are carrying heavy burdens, and I will give you rest (Matthew 11:28), say,
Jesus, I cast all my anxieties on you.

OPTION 2 — Spend time deep breathing.*
After 10 minutes or more, open your eyes and stretch your arms out, palms down. Imagine all the sources of stress in your life dropping from you into God's able hands, as you pray,
Jesus, I cast all my anxieties on you.

*For more information see the Introduction.

BLESSING
May the Lord be my defender, my protector, my refuge, and my rest. Amen

Blessing of Encouragement in Times of Prejudice or Discrimination

PREPARATION Light a single candle* as a sign of God's presence. You will need a Bible, a piece of paper and a pencil/pen. You may also bring a small symbol of God's presence (a cross, a rock, a Bible verse) that you can carry with you after the blessing.

WELCOME

For everything there is a season,
and a time for every matter under heaven.
Welcome to this time for claiming God's love and justice.

OPENING PRAYER

O God, you care for the oppressed and heal the brokenhearted. Be with me/us now as a light in the midst of this darkness. Amen

BIBLE TEXT

. . . for in Christ Jesus you are all children of God through faith . . . There is no longer Jew or Greek, there is no longer slave or free, there is no longer male and female;
for all of you are one in Christ Jesus. Galatians 3:26, 28

REFLECTION

Share or write in a journal* about your experience of prejudice or discrimination. What happened? How did it make you feel? What made you angry? What was hurtful? As a reminder that God is present with those who are suffering persecution, read all of Psalm 56 or vv. 5-11.

RITUAL ACTION

In Psalm 56:7, the psalmist gives us permission to be angry, to want to get even, and to ask God to justly deal with the people who have hurt us. On your paper write this prayer:
O God of justice, I am angry at (name) for (name of behavior). Trusting your justice, I ask you to deal with them, so I can be free from hate. (If you are doing this blessing with children, write out their prayer for them.)
Speak or yell your prayer aloud. Then tear up the paper and toss the pieces into the air, saying, **God, I give you my anger.**

After releasing your anger, remember that Jesus calls on us to *pray for those who persecute us* (Matthew 5:44).

Pray this prayer or one of your own. **Dear God, you are a God of love and not hate. Shine your light into the hearts and minds of all who hurt others, so they will change their hurtful ways and learn how to love as you love us. Take away all fear, help me forgive, and give me courage to stand strong in the face of prejudice and discrimination. Amen**

*For more information see the Introduction.

BLESSING

May you remember these words from God:
You are precious in my sight, and honored, and I love you . . . Do not fear, for I am with you. Isaiah 43:4-5

Blessing for Moving Out and Moving On

PREPARATION This blessing is for use when a person or family is moving out of a home. You might want to do it the night before you leave, or when the house has been emptied and cleaned, as a final good-bye to a place that represents a stage of life. If you can find a candle* and matches, do the blessing as suggested. Otherwise, simply speak the words and imagine the light.

WELCOME
For everything there is a season,
and a time for every matter under heaven.
Welcome to this time of remembering and moving on.

PRAYER
Gracious God, you gave me/us a home in which to grow and rest, to find shelter and experience the many joys and sorrows of life. Thank you for the blessings of this place and what it has meant to all who have lived here. May this home be a blessing to those who come after me/us. Amen

BIBLE TEXT
The Lord will keep your going out and your coming in
from this time on and forevermore. Psalm 121:8

REFLECTION AND RITUAL ACTION
OPTION 1 — Light your candle and move from room to room. If you are alone, let the light of the candle shed light on your memories, bringing healing to the sorrows and revealing the joys. If you are with others, share any memory you are comfortable sharing.

Then speak this blessing on the room,
I/We give to you, O God, all my/our moments in this room and say good-bye. May this room be filled with your light and life for all who will live here.

OPTION 2 — Light the candle. In each room of the house write in a journal* or share your response to the following statements:
A joyful memory or meaningful moment I had in this room was . . .
A moment of hurt or pain experienced in this room was . . .

Then speak this blessing on the room:
I/We give to you, O God, all my/our moments in this room and say good-bye. May this room be filled with your light and life for all who will live here.

SONG
Sing or say, *As You Go on Our Way,* (p. 84). (Use the appropriate variation.)

*For more information see the Introduction.

BLESSING
May God watch over all who move from their homes, blessing them with strength and vision to create new homes. Amen

Blessing during a Job Transition

PREPARATION People can expect to change jobs several times during their lives. Sometimes these transitions are forced and very painful. Other times they are more joyful. But in either case they involve change and the unknown. This blessing can be done alone or with all those who are affected by this change. Set out a begging bowl* and fill a blessing cup.*

WELCOME

For everything there is a season,
and a time for every matter under heaven.
Welcome to this time for change and new vision.

PRAYER

O God of our labor, we pray that all who follow you will find work that fulfills their calling and your purpose in their lives and in the life of the world. Amen

BIBLE TEXT

We know that all things work together for good for those who love God, who are called according to God's purpose.
Romans 8: 28

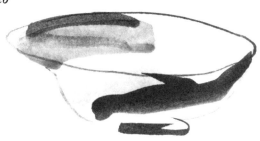

REFLECTION

Whether the termination of your past job was voluntary or involuntary, it involves regrets and loss for you, for your family, and for others close to you. Share or write in a journal*about that sadness, anger, and/or loss. If others are present, ask them to share their feelings as well.

Clinging to the promise that all things work together for good, share or write in a journal about your hope for a new way of life, new priorities, and a new vision this transition can bring.

RITUAL ACTION

Hold the begging bowl and say these words,
Dear Lord, please give me all I need, as I move through this time of change. Amen
Give everyone a chance to hold the bowl and pray.

Then pass the blessing cup, repeating the Bible verse to one another. *We know that all things work together for good for those who love God, who are called according to God's purpose* (Romans 8: 28). You may also wish to write this verse on a piece of paper ahead of time, and then carry it with you throughout the transition.

*For more information see the Introduction.

BLESSING

May God who loves you and calls you into meaningful work, walk with you, bringing all things together for good. Amen

Blessing for the Empty Nest

WELCOME

For everything there is a season,
and a time for every matter under heaven.
Welcome to this time of letting go and transition.

PRAYER

O God, you sent your only Son into the world. Give me/us the grace to let my/our child(ren) go, trusting that you will complete the work you have begun in each of us. Amen

BIBLE TEXT

You will do everything you have promised; Lord, your love is eternal. Complete the work that you have begun.
Psalm 138:8 (TEV)

I am confident of this, that the one who began a good work among you will bring it to completion by the day of Jesus Christ. Philippians 1:6

REFLECTION

Share or write in a journal* about the lives of each child in the family, noting ways in which each has grown and developed over the years. Pray this prayer for each one:

Thank you, God, for all the changes and growth that have happened in (name)'s life. Please complete the work you have begun. Your love is eternal, and you will do everything you have promised. Amen

Then think about yourself/selves. In this time of transition, what do you need from your significant relationships (spouse, children, church community . . .)? Share or write in a journal your needs and how you might find ways to meet them.

The empty nest indicates it is time to re-imagine the role of parent. Share or write in a journal new images or ideas for this new role. (For instance, now I can be more like a friend, a colleague, an older sister/brother . . .)

You, along with your children, are a work of God's hands, a work in process. Dream of all you can be. Share or write in a journal specific areas of your life you now want to explore. Pray for yourself/selves the prayer you prayed for your children.

RITUAL ACTION

Drink from the blessing cup, saying, **Bless those who have left this nest, and bless this space, giving it and me/us new beginnings.** (This blessing may be done in every room of the house.)

*For more information see the Introduction.

BLESSING

May God, whose wings spread wide, covering and protecting all nests, bless me/us, completing in me/us all that God has begun.
Amen

Blessing Our Mid-Life Body Changes

PREPARATION   Invite friends to celebrate with you. Place a large candle in the center of the table representing all you have been and can be. Find pictures or other symbols representing each decade of your life. Set them out with a small candle* next to each one. Light the candles and fill a blessing cup.* Adapt the blessing if you are alone.

WELCOME
For everything there is a season,
and a time for every matter under heaven.
Welcome to this celebration of changes in my body.

PRAYER
O God, who formed us in our mother's womb and continues to form us all our lives, be with us during this time when the changes in our bodies mark the passing of years. Bless us with your wisdom. Amen

BIBLE TEXT
Happy are those who find wisdom, and those who get understanding, for her income is better than silver . . . She is more precious than jewels, and nothing you desire can compare with her. Long life is in her right hand; in her left hand are riches and honor. Her ways are ways of pleasantness, and all her paths are peace. She is a tree of life to those who lay hold of her; those who hold her fast are called happy. Proverbs 3: 13-18

REFLECTION
Share or write in a journal* about your body in each decade of your life. What joy have you experienced through your body?

What have you struggled with in relationship to your body? What parts of your body have you loved and do you love the most? How do you feel about the current changes happening in your body?

Many cultures in the world accord the status of wise woman or wise man to those past mid-life. This is based on the observation that only through a variety of life experiences, hard struggle, and reflection on that struggle, does one become wise.

Having reflected on your body through the decades of your life, share or write in a journal your thoughts about these questions. **What wisdom have I gained through my body experiences and changes? What wisdom would I want to pass on to younger women/men? How can I treat my body with the reverence and respect it deserves?**

RITUAL ACTION
Pass the blessing cup, saying a blessing for the person experiencing changes. Conclude with this prayer: **Holy One, you have made our bodies temples of your Holy Spirit. Bless (name)'s body--its wisdom, its strength, its beauty. May she/he treat it tenderly and with reverence now and always. Amen**

*For more information see the Introduction.

BLESSING
May we be filled with gratitude and Holy Wisdom. Amen

Blessing for Retirement

PREPARATION Invite others to celebrate with you. Set out a tall candle.* Also, if you have them, set out a calendar and a clock, representing the new gift of time you have in retirement. Light the candle and fill a blessing cup.*

WELCOME
For everything there is a season,
and a time for every matter under heaven.
Welcome to this time for new beginnings.

PRAYER
O God, you called Abraham and Sarah away from all they knew and into a distant land, where they were blessed to be a blessing. Empower those who have been blessed with a lifetime of work to be a blessing in retirement. Amen

BIBLE TEXT
By faith Abraham obeyed when he was called to set out for a place that he was to receive as an inheritance; and he set out, not knowing where he was going.
Hebrews 11:8

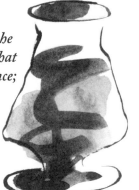

REFLECTION
When Abraham and Sarah set out for the promised land, they brought with them all the skills and values they had learned during their lives. Look back on your work life outside of the home and reflect on the following questions:

What skills, values, and wisdom have you gained?
What are you proud of?
What would you have done differently?
What blessings have you been given that you can now use to bless others?

Share or write in a journal* your responses. Invite those gathered to share their insights as well.

RITUAL ACTION
The person retiring drinks from the blessing cup, as those gathered say a blessing of their own or the following blessing:
(Name), may God lead and guide you into the fullness of this new stage of life, so that you will continue to be a blessing to others.

*For more information see the Introduction.

BLESSING
May we all walk boldly into the future, blessed to be a blessing. Amen

Blessing Our Loss of Independence

PREPARATION None of us is ever truly independent, and yet there are life circumstances, most often but not always the result of aging, that force us into recognizing our dependence in dramatic and often painful and frustrating ways — loss of a driver's license, loss of the ability to leave home, to walk, to leave one's bed. Option 1 is for a friend or family member planning the blessing for a loved one, who has lost his or her independence. Fill a blessing cup.*
Option 2 is for those planning their own blessing.

WELCOME

For everything there is a season,
and a time for every matter under heaven.
Welcome to this time of grieving our losses and claiming the possibilities that remain.

PRAYER

Tender God, sustainer of our lives, I/we come to you this day, thanking you for all that has been and asking for your strength and your grace for all that is to come. Amen

BIBLE TEXT

Are not five sparrows sold for two pennies? Yet not one of them is forgotten in God's sight. But even the hairs of your head are all counted. Do not be afraid; you are of more value than many sparrows. Luke 12:6-7

REFLECTION

Share or write in a journal* your thoughts about the losses you are experiencing.
I feel _____ about my loss of independence.
What do I miss most from my past life? Why?
What things do I wish I had done differently? Why?
What part of that life gave me the most joy? Why?

Now, think about the future.
What can I still do that is of value?
Who needs my prayers, my support, my love?
What help do I need in order to do what I can still do?

RITUAL ACTION

OPTION 1 — Pass the blessing cup and say a blessing of your own or these words,
(Name), I honor your life, rejoicing in the value you have, and I pray that God will sustain and nurture you so you will continue to find meaning and joy in life.

OPTION 2 — Make the sign of the cross* on your forehead and on your heart as a way of claiming the gift of life and hope for the future.

*For more information see the Introduction.

BLESSING
May we feel the tender arms of God holding us, loving us, and giving us hope. Amen

SEASONS OF OUR RELATIONSHIPS

Blessing of Friendship

PREPARATION   This blessing can be used for a reunion of old friends, after the restoration of a friendship, or anytime a particular friendship needs celebrating. Invite your friend or friends to a quiet place. Share a meal with them, if appropriate. Fill a blessing cup.*

WELCOME
For everything there is a season,
and a time for every matter under heaven.
Welcome to this celebration of the gift of friendship.

PRAYER
God of love, we thank you for all who make life richer through the gift of friendship and especially for (name[s]). We are grateful for our shared memory and history, for the gift of knowing and being known, and for friendship that binds our hearts together.
In Jesus' name we pray.   Amen

BIBLE TEXT
Some friends play at friendship,
but a true friend sticks closer than
one's nearest kin.
Proverbs 18:24

REFLECTION
Share with each other a conversation, an event, or an aspect of your relationship that has particular significance for you.
Then ask:
Why is this friendship so special to you?
What do you need from each other to encourage the friendship to grow?
What do you need from each other to help you to grow as individuals?
Share your responses.

RITUAL ACTION
Pass the blessing cup, saying these words,
Thank you for sharing your life with me!

Some people (especially pre-adolescents and teenagers) find exchanging gifts with friends meaningful. Consider making or buying something that represents your friendship (a friendship bracelet, jewelry, matching clothes, plants . . .). Exchange the items with these words,
Thank you for being my friend.

*For more information see the Introduction.

BLESSING
May the love of Christ continue to bind us together in joy and sorrow, through laughter and tears, with love and hope
for years to come. Amen

Blessing for Revealing Our Hidden Selves

PREPARATION This blessing is for those times when one person is ready to reveal, admit, or confess to another or others something that has previously been kept secret. Write a letter to friends/family revealing the parts of yourself you no longer want to hide, but do not mail it. Include how you got to this point, your feelings about telling this truth, and your hopes for the future. Prepare a safe place, setting out objects or symbols that give you strength and courage, including a single unlit candle.*

Invite friends/family with whom you want to share this part of yourself. While the truth, indeed, sets us free, it can be joyful or painful, or both! You are encouraged to adapt the blessing to your particular situation in whatever way is appropriate. Remember that the focus of the truth telling is on you and your experience, not on blaming others. The power of this blessing comes in claiming God's power in your life, claiming your own power, and taking new responsibility for your life, regardless of the past actions, mistakes or failings of yourself or others.

WELCOME

For everything there is a season,
and a time for every matter under heaven.
Welcome to this time of truth telling.

PRAYER

Lover of Truth and Spirit of Courage, bless this time of truth telling with your presence and your guidance. Amen

BIBLE TEXT

Then you will know the truth, and the truth will set you free.
John 8:32

REVEALING

Read the letter to those gathered, asking them to listen in silence. When you have finished reading, allow time for responses or move on to one of the ritual actions.

RITUAL ACTION

OPTION 1 — The truth teller lights the candle and says, **Thank you for allowing me to shed light on the hidden places in my life. I pray that you will grow to (accept, forgive, celebrate with . . .) me, so that we can move forward together with greater honesty and freedom.**

OPTION 2 — Light the candle and ask friends/family to gather around you and place their hands on your head and shoulders. Invite those surrounding you to offer prayers, and/or ask one person to read the following blessing: **Thank you, (name), for having the courage to speak your truth and for trusting us to hear it. May this truth telling be the beginning of new freedom for you and for us all. Amen**

*For more information see the Introduction.

BLESSING

The Lord bless you and keep you. The Lord's face shine on you and be gracious to you. The Lord look upon you with favor,
and give you peace. **Amen** (Numbers 6:24-26)

Blessing for Forgiveness and Reconciliation

PREPARATION This blessing can be initiated by the person needing to be forgiven or by a third party concerned about a current issue. Prepare a safe place by putting a cross and candle* on the table. Find a fire-resistant bowl in which you can burn paper (unless restricted by fire codes). Also set out small pieces of paper and pencils/pens on a table. Light the candle.

WELCOME

For everything there is a season,
and a time for every matter under heaven.
Welcome to this time of forgiveness and reconciliation.

PRAYER

Dear God, you have called us to confess our sins and to forgive as we have been forgiven by you. Give to us an open mind, a forgiving heart, and a compassionate response. Amen

BIBLE TEXT

As far as the east is from the west, so far God removes our sins from us.
Psalm 103:12 (TEV)

REFLECTION

Write down on the paper the sins you want to confess. Take time to think of those things you have done and things you have not done for which you need forgiveness. Share your sins with the other. Give the other time to express hurt, anger, fear, relief, or any other emotion caused by the revelation.

If you are the third party, suggest that both people write out the ways they have failed. Do the reflection and ritual action for one person before focusing on the other. If more than two people are involved, repeat the reflection and ritual action for as many people as wish to confess something.

RITUAL ACTION

Take the piece of paper with your sins listed on it and give it to the other person, saying, **I'm sorry I wronged you. I will try to change my ways. And I ask you to please forgive me.**

If the wronged person finds it in his or her heart to forgive you now, ask him or her to light the paper with the candle flame, and put it in the bowl to burn to ashes, saying, **I forgive you.** If you are not allowed to burn, tear the paper to shreds.

If the person cannot forgive at this time, after he or she has left, burn or shred the paper as a sign that you are forgiving yourself.

*For more information see the Introduction.

BLESSING

May we experience the great gift forgiveness brings--reconciliation of our relationship with ourselves, others, and God. Amen

48

Blessing for a Reunion of Family or Friends

PREPARATION All present should bring pictures and/or stories of life experiences that have occurred since you have been together last. Light one large candle* and surround it with small unlit candles, one for each person present. Fill a blessing cup.* If the group is large, divide into small groups for the reflection.

WELCOME

For everything there is a season,
and a time for every matter under heaven.
Welcome to this time of celebration for friends/family gathering together again.

PRAYER

Creator and Sustainer of us all, we thank you for the blessing of being able to gather together and for walking with us on our journeys. Help us share openly and celebrate the blessing of each person's life. Amen

BIBLE TEXT

Above all, clothe yourselves with love, which binds everything together in perfect harmony. And let the peace of Christ rule in your hearts, to which indeed you were called in the one body. And be thankful.
Colossians 3:14-15

Rejoice with those who rejoice, weep with those who weep.
Live in harmony with one another.
Romans 12:15-16a

REFLECTION

If introductions are necessary, make them at this time. Then ask each to share responses to one or more of the following sentence starters:

Since the last time we were together, the events in my life for which I am most thankful are . . .
My disappointments have been . . .
My hopes for the future are . . .

After each person shares, ask him or her to light a small candle. When the sharing is complete, say,
We rejoice with those who rejoice and weep with those who weep. May the light from each life burn brightly during this time together.

RITUAL ACTION

After everyone has shared, pass the blessing cup, saying a blessing of your own, or,
Thank you all for the light you bring to my life.

*For more information see the Introduction.

BLESSING

May God bless this time, giving us love for each other, harmony among us, and grateful hearts. Amen

Blessing of Intentional Relationships

PREPARATION This blessing is for two or more people who formally pledge to journey together for a time (for instance, co-workers, a spiritual director and directee, roommates, a mentor and mentee, prayer partners . . .). Place a large candle* and a small candle for each person present in the center of the table. Light the large candle symbolizing the presence of the Holy Spirit. Set out paper and pencils/pens.

WELCOME

For everything there is a season,
and a time for every matter under heaven.
Welcome to this time for celebrating the
life-giving power of our relationship(s).

PRAYER

(To be read by one person or together.)
Gracious God, thank you for blessing our lives with the gift of each other. Give us what we need to be faithful to you and to the covenant we will make, that our lives may be enriched with mutual growth through Christ. Amen

BIBLE TEXT

If then there is any encouragement in Christ, any consolation from love, any sharing in the Spirit, any compassion and sympathy, make my joy complete: be of the same mind, having the same love, being in full accord and of one mind.

Do nothing from selfish ambition or conceit, but in humility regard others as better than yourselves. Let each of you look not to your own interests, but to the interests of others.
Philippians 2:1-4

REFLECTION

Share with each other the hopes and concerns you have for the relationship(s). Talk about what you are willing to invest in the relationship(s), for instance: time, energy, prayer . . .

RITUAL ACTION

Write a covenant for your relationship(s). Include expectations for the amount of time you will spend together, a commitment to pray for each other, hopes for the growth of your relationship(s), a commitment to be responsible and compassionate toward the other, and anything else that is necessary.

When the covenant is agreed upon, each person signs the paper and lights one small candle, saying,
May God bless us and the covenant we have made.

*For more information see the Introduction.

BLESSING
May God's love for us be reflected in our commitment to each other. Amen

Blessing of a Marriage

PREPARATION This blessing may be done at the rehearsal dinner or at another gathering of close family and friends before or after the wedding. Fill a blessing cup.* Someone other than the couple may wish to lead the blessing.

WELCOME
For everything there is a season,
and a time for every matter under heaven.
Welcome to this time for blessing the marriage of (name) and (name).

PRAYER
Maker and giver of love, bless us with your presence here as we gather to celebrate your love shown through (name) and (name). May their union be blessed by you so that together they may be a blessing to others. Amen

BIBLE TEXT
The Lord said to Abram, "I will make of you a great nation, and I will bless you, and make your name great, so that you will be a blessing." Genesis 12:2

REFLECTION/RITUAL ACTION
Pass the blessing cup, sharing a blessing for the couple, along with other appropriate stories or memories. Suggestions for blessings are:

My hope for you as a couple is . . .
You have blessed my life by . . .
May you bless your community by . . .
God has blessed you with . . .
May you use these gifts to . . .

When all who wish have offered a blessing, the couple receives the cup, each taking a sip, symbolically drinking in the blessings each person has spoken.

The couple may respond with the following prayer:
Gracious God, we give you thanks for all the people gathered here and for all the blessings spoken here. With them we offer ourselves and our relationship to you, that you may use us for your purposes, and that we may be a blessing for all our days to come. Amen

*For more information see the Introduction.

51

BLESSING
In our love and in our lives, may we be blessed to be a blessing. Amen

Blessing of a Pregnancy

PREPARATION Gather together the parent(s) of the unborn child, family and friends. Set out one large and many small candles.* Light the large candle. Option 1 is for a group gathered with the expectant parent(s). Option 2 is for a mother doing this blessing alone. Adjust as necessary for other situations.

WELCOME

For everything there is a season,
and a time for every matter under heaven.
Welcome to this time of great anticipation.

PRAYER

Creating God, the miracle of life has begun anew. Bless me/us in these coming months with joy in each day, with hope for the future, with trust in your presence. Amen

BIBLE TEXT

You formed my inward parts. You knit me together in my mother's womb. Psalm 139:13

REFLECTION

OPTION 1 — Pregnancy can be a time of both great expectation and fear. Ask the parent(s) to share with those gathered their fears, as well as their hopes.

OPTION 2 — Write in a journal* about your hopes and your fears.

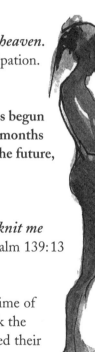

RITUAL ACTION

OPTION 1 — Invite all to share a hope they have for the baby and the baby's family as they light a candle.

Then ask those gathered to visualize* every part of the unborn baby's body from the toes of the feet to the hairs on the head. Pray this prayer or have those gathered pray a prayer of their own. If appropriate, those gathered may place their hands on the mother's stomach while praying.

Creator God, knit together this tiny child's body and mind, its heart and soul, tenderly caring for each part, and bring this child safely to birth. Amen

OPTION 2 — Light a candle for each of the hopes you have for your baby. Focus on the light, and imagine it as the creative light of God. Then visualize* that light touching every part of your baby's body. Pray a prayer of your own or the prayer in option 1.

Then spend time writing in a journal about all the ways you pledge to take care of your own body so your baby can have the best possible chance for a whole life.

*For more information see the Introduction.

BLESSING
May God be diligently at work knitting this new life together during these days and months of hopeful waiting. Amen

Blessing after a Stillbirth or Miscarriage

PREPARATION Use option 1 if the blessing is initiated by the parent(s) experiencing the loss. Use option 2 if family or friends initiate the blessing. Light a candle* to symbolize God's presence. Fill a blessing cup.*

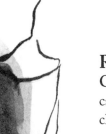

WELCOME
For everything there is a season,
and time for every matter under heaven
Welcome to this time of grieving the loss of this life and the lost hopes and dreams.

PRAYER
Gracious God, trusting that your love and compassion surround all who struggle with loss and grief, with questions and confusion, I/we pray for courage to say good-bye to this life, known fully by you, and to all the hopes and dreams I/we had for this child. In Jesus' name, Amen

BIBLE TEXT
But now thus says the Lord, the one who created you, O Jacob, the one who formed you, O Israel: Do not fear, for I have redeemed you. I have called you by name, you are mine. Isaiah 43:1

REFLECTION
Share or write in a journal* using these sentence starters:
The hopes and dreams I had for this child were . . .
I feel saddest about . . . What I don't understand is . . .
All present are encouraged to share their thoughts and feelings.

RITUAL ACTION
OPTION 1 — God knows us even before we are born and has called us by name. If you had not thought of a name, call the child, God's Little One.

Then, holding the blessing cup say, **I/we name you, (name), and we drink from the blessing cup to honor your life and brief presence among us.** Drink from the cup.

Then make the sign of the cross* and say,
(Name), into God's hands we commend your spirit.

OPTION 2 — Encourage the parent(s) to do option 1. Then, ask the parent(s) what they will need from you in the days and weeks ahead. Ask each person present to offer a service or support for the parent(s), such as:

I will pray for you daily; I will clean your house; I will call those who need calling; I will make some food; I will . . .

Then pass the blessing cup, saying a blessing of your own, or, **I/We love you, (name of parent[s]). You are not alone.**

*For more information see the Introduction.

53

BLESSING
May (name of parent[s]) find comfort in the One who called us by name and keeps us forever. Amen

Blessing of a Birth or Adoption

PREPARATION Bring together the child, parent(s), and any other person who will be part of the circle of love for this child. Light a candle* and set out a begging bowl.* If there is more than one child, each child's life can be celebrated separately.

WELCOME
For everything there is a season,
and a time for every matter under heaven.
Welcome to this time for celebrating this gift to our family and to the human family.

PRAYER
O God of life, thank you for the gift of this child, for all (name) will bring to our lives, for trusting us with his/her care, for giving us the opportunity to love this child deeply. Help us to grow as a family and to always give thanks for one another. Grant us patience in times of weariness and delight in (name) at each stage of his/her growth. Amen

BIBLE TEXT
For what thanksgiving can we render to God for you,
for all the joy which we feel for your sake.
1 Thessalonians 3:9 (RSV)

REFLECTION
As a family, you are now beginning a whole new phase of life with the addition of a new child. Reflect on and share the things that will change because of this birth or adoption. Give thanks for the life you had before the arrival of this child. (Omit this if the child is old enough to understand.)

Now finish these sentences and share your thoughts.
My hope for this child is . . .
My hope for our new life together is . . .

RITUAL ACTION
The mother or father now holds the begging bowl and prays,
O God, you have given us this child. Now please give us whatever we need to help (name) live a full life as your beloved child. Amen If the child is adopted, add this prayer,
We pray your blessings on (name)'s birth parents and thank them for this incredible gift. Amen

Then, if the child is an infant, hold him or her. If it is an older child, have the group form a circle and ask the child to stand in the center while those gathered place their hands on his or her head. Pray or ask all gathered to pray,
Thank you, God, for this precious gift.

Then, if you are alone say, **I'm so glad you're here.**
Or, have the group say, **We're so grateful you're here.**

*For more information see the Introduction.

BLESSING
May the joy of this moment sustain us in our lifetime of growing together. Amen

Blessing for Wedding Anniversaries

PREPARATION Find and place in the center of a table mementos, pictures, wedding vows
or anything that symbolizes your life together. Set out a single candle* (the unity candle if one was used).
Light the candle. Fill a blessing cup.* Adapt the blessing if you are planning a celebration for someone else.

WELCOME
For everything there is a season,
and a time for every matter under heaven.
Welcome to this time for celebrating
commitment and love.

PRAYER
Source of all love, we thank you for the
(number) years we have been joined together
as one. May you continue to bless our lives and
help us to forgive as you have forgiven us.
Strengthen us during difficult times, and grant
us a maturing love as we continue this journey
of life together. Amen

BIBLE TEXT
And now faith, hope, and love abide, these three; and the
greatest of these is love. 1 Corinthians 13:13

REFLECTION
Thinking back over the years of your marriage and
your wedding day, complete the following sentences:
I am grateful for . . .
I am sorry for . . .

Thinking to the years ahead, complete these sentences:
I am concerned about . . .
I am hopeful for . . .

RITUAL ACTION
Hold hands, look into each other's eyes, repeat your wedding
vows and/or say, one at a time,
I promise for another year to love you as fully as possible,
treat you as gently as possible, and journey with you
as joyfully as possible.
Drink from the blessing cup.

SONG
Sing or play one of your favorite songs from your wedding day.

*For more information see the Introduction.

55

BLESSING
May we grow in faith, live in hope, and abide in love as we enter another year of marriage. Amen

Blessing for Important Conversations

PREPARATION   There are times in every relationship when it is necessary to have important conversations. These could be talks about sexuality with children, about job loss or transition with the family, about the death of a loved one . . . Gather those involved in the conversation in a circle or around a table. Place a candle* in the center of the room or table and as you light the candle say, **The truth of Christ is present here.**

WELCOME
For everything there is a season,
and a time for every matter under heaven.
Welcome to this time of openness and honesty.

PRAYER
Holy Wisdom, through your words you brought this universe into being and those words continue to be truth and life for all who believe in you. May the words spoken today follow your lead so that honesty is grounded in compassion, expectations are cradled in love, and fear is tempered by trust in you. Amen

BIBLE TEXT
Thoughtless words can wound as deeply as any sword,
but wise words can heal. Proverbs 12:18 (TEV)

REFLECTION
Begin the conversation with one person stating the issue(s) at hand or explaining the subject. Allow time for questions and input from all present. Listen to one another carefully without interruption. Keep the discussion open until the conversation has reached its conclusion. As the conversation progresses, even if it takes a difficult turn, it is important to see the others in the room as Jesus sees us all — persons deserving respect and love.

If the conversation is among several people, it might be wise to have a talking stick or stone. Only the person holding the stick or stone can talk. When one person is through talking, he or she passes the object on to the next person. This is one way to ensure people will not be interrupted and everyone will have a chance to talk.

RITUAL ACTION
When the conversation is completed, join hands and pray the following prayer or the squeeze prayer,*
God of truth and life, thank you
for the time we have spent together,
for the honest conversation,
and for the insights gained. Be with us
as we explore new understandings and new ways
of relating. In the name of Jesus, your Son, we pray.
Amen

Conclude with the Lord's Prayer (p. 84).

*For more information see the Introduction.

BLESSING
May the words spoken today heal our hearts, calm our concerns, and give us hope for the future. Amen

Blessing after the Ending or Changing of a Relationship

PREPARATION This blessing is intended to help an individual or family after a divorce, separation, or change of relationship (perhaps due to Alzheimer's disease or another illness). During these difficult times, sometimes we need to pray for ourselves (option 1). Sometimes we need to let go of the other person (option 2). Sometimes we need both. Use the parts of the blessing that are helpful. The blessing may also be repeated over time as often as is desired. Light a single candle* to symbolize God's presence with you, and place a begging bowl* next to it.

WELCOME
For everything there is a season,
and a time for every matter under heaven.
Welcome to this time for remembering God's abiding presence during difficult life passages.

PRAYER
God, I/we know you are always present, but bring awareness of your presence now, during this journey into the unknown. Amen

BIBLE TEXT
For I am convinced that neither death, nor life . . . nor things present, nor things to come, nor powers, nor height, nor depth, nor anything else in all creation, will be able to separate us from the love of God in Christ Jesus our Lord.
Romans 8:38-39

REFLECTION
Change in a relationship produces a wide range of emotions. Write in a journal * or share how you feel about the ending or changing of this relationship. These sentence starters might be helpful: **I miss . . . I'm angry about . . . I'm sad about . . . I have hope for . . .**

RITUAL ACTION
OPTION 1 — Speak this blessing as if God were saying it to you. *But now thus says the Lord . . . Do not fear, for I have redeemed you; I have called you by name, you are mine . . . Do not fear for I am with you. Amen* (Isaiah 43:1-2, 5)

OPTION 2 — One person or all may read this blessing: (Name), child of God, I want you to know that (I miss you/I love you/I forgive you . . .), and I entrust you to God's care. *The Lord bless you and keep you. The Lord's face shine on you and be gracious to you. The Lord look upon you with favor, and give you peace.* **Amen** (Numbers 6:24-26)

CLOSING PRAYER
Hold the begging bowl and say, **God, I know I am not alone. You are with me. Fill me with all I need for the day. Amen**

*For more information see the Introduction.

BLESSING
May the love of God in Christ Jesus surround and fill us now and always. Amen

Blessing for a Blended Family

PREPARATION Find a quiet time and place when all members of the new family can be together. Place an unlit candle* on a table. Have small (6 inch) pieces of yarn or string (preferably of different colors) available, one for each member of the family. Set them next to the candle.

WELCOME

For everything there is a season,
and a time for every matter under heaven.
Welcome to this time of growth toward unity.

PRAYER

God of life and love, you have called us into unity with you and with each other. Remind us always that, though we have come from different places and experiences, your love for us and our growing love for one another can bind our hearts together and give us a common purpose.
Amen

BIBLE TEXT

As God's chosen ones, holy and beloved, clothe yourselves with compassion, kindness, humility, meekness, and patience. Bear with one another and, if anyone has a complaint against another, forgive each other; just as the Lord has forgiven you, so you must also forgive. Above all, clothe yourselves with love, which binds everything together in perfect harmony.
Colossians 3:12-14

REFLECTION

Invite every person who is old enough to complete these sentences and share their responses:

Right now I am feeling . . .
When I think about this family's future, the thing I worry about the most is . . .
My greatest hope for this family is . . .

RITUAL ACTION

Ask each person to take a piece of string/yarn. Beginning with the parents, one by one tie the pieces of yarn together until they form a circle. Lay the circle on the table and place the candle within the circle you have just created. Light it and say, **May the light of God's love always shine among us.**

When the ritual action is completed, put the circle of yarn in a visible place.

*For more information see the Introduction.

BLESSING

May our hearts be bound together by the light of God's love among us, and through the growing love we have for each other.
Amen

Blessing for Letting Go of a Loved One Near Death

PREPARATION Talk to your loved one about this blessing, if possible, to prepare him or her.
Gather all family and friends for whom such a blessing would be important.
If you want communion at this time, ask a clergy to be present. If not, fill a blessing cup.*

WELCOME

For everything there is a season,
and a time for every matter under heaven.
Welcome to this time of saying good-bye to our loved one.

PRAYER

Precious Lord, we come to you today with heavy hearts and
minds. We also come thanking you for the life of (name).
Fill us with your Spirit who brings comfort in our grief,
strength for the days ahead, and hope of eternal life,
through Jesus Christ our Lord. Amen

BIBLE TEXT

Do not let your hearts be troubled. Believe in God.
Believe also in me. In my Father's house there are many
dwelling places. If it were not so, would I have told you that
I go to prepare a place for you? And if I go and prepare a
place for you, I will come again and will take you to myself,
so that where I am, there you may be also.
John 14:1-3

REFLECTION

Allow each person time to stand near the dying loved one and
say, **I love you,** and, **Good-bye,** or anything else that seems
important. If the dying person can talk, encourage a response.

RITUAL ACTION

If there is a clergy present and communion is desired, celebrate
the sacrament at this time. If not, pass the blessing cup, saying,
You are held by God's strong hand.

Surround your loved one in a circle, holding hands, including
the hands of the loved one. Sing or say a favorite hymn such as
Precious Lord, or *Beautiful Savior.*
Then sing or say to your loved one,
As You Go on Your Way, (p. 84).

Finally, let the hands of the loved one go.

SONG

Sing or say, *As You Go on Your Way,* (p. 84), using variation 2.

*For more information see the Introduction.

59

BLESSING
May God's almighty and tender hand hold each of us now and into eternity. Go in peace. Amen

Blessing and Sending after a Funeral

PREPARATION This blessing is intended for that time after the funeral of a loved one when close friends and family are gathered together. Set out a begging bowl.*

WELCOME
For everything there is a season,
and a time for every matter under heaven.
Welcome to this time of entrusting the coming days
to God's care.

PRAYER
O Lord, our Creator and Redeemer, you have given us the circle of life on earth as well as everlasting life with you. Now that we have released (name) to be with you forever, we pray that you will give us courage to live out our days confident of your resurrected power. Amen

BIBLE TEXT
The Lord is my shepherd, I shall not want; he makes me lie down in green pastures. He leads me beside still waters; he restores my soul. He leads me in the paths of righteousness for his name's sake. Even though I walk through the valley of the shadow of death, I fear no evil; for thou art with me; thy rod and thy staff, they comfort me. Thou preparest a table before me in the presence of my enemies; thou anointest my head with oil, my cup overflows. Surely goodness and mercy shall follow me all the days of my life, and I shall dwell in the house of the Lord for ever. Psalm 23 (RSV)

REFLECTION
Take a few moments to think about your loved one's life. Share words or stories about your loved one — humorous moments, comforting memories . . . You may also wish to share any worries or fears you have about the days to come.

RITUAL ACTION
After sharing, have each person hold the begging bowl and say, I ask you, God, to give me what I need in the days ahead.

SONG
Sing or say a favorite song such as *Amazing Grace* or *As You Go on Your Way,* (p. 84), using variation 2.

*For more information see the Introduction.

BLESSING
May we go in peace, knowing we are fully surrounded by God's love, and we will all dwell in the house of the Lord forever.
Amen

Blessing for the Disposition of Ashes

PREPARATION Ahead of time, determine with other members of the family whether the ashes will be buried, scattered, or placed in a chosen site. Gather family members and/or friends. Bring the urn or box containing the ashes.

WELCOME

For everything there is a season,
and a time for every matter under heaven.
Welcome to this time of remembering (name) and claiming the hope of life eternal through Christ.

PRAYER

God of beginnings and endings, we thank you for blessing our lives with the gift of (name). Bless also our memories--times of joy and of sorrow--that shaped our lives together. Release us from our regrets. Turn our grief into joy. Help us to trust your promise that in life and death we are yours. Amen

BIBLE TEXT

Then the Lord God formed a person from the dust of the ground, and breathed into their nostrils the breath of life; and the person became a living being. Genesis 2:7

. . . you are dust and to dust you shall return. Genesis 3:19

REFLECTION

Share or write in a journal*your memories of your loved one. When all who care to speak have spoken, say,
Grateful for (name)'s presence in our lives, we entrust him/her to God's never failing love.

RITUAL ACTION

Make the sign of the cross* over the ashes and then scatter, bury, or place them, saying these words:

The Lord bless you and keep you.
The Lord's face shine on you and be gracious to you.
The Lord look upon you with favor, and give you peace.
Amen (Numbers 6:24-26)

Then repeat these words, for the people gathered, changing the "you" to "us" — *The Lord bless us . . .*

61

*For more information see the Introduction.

BLESSING

May we live in hope that in Christ we are united now and forever with all who have gone before us. Amen

Blessing for Anniversary of a Death

PREPARATION Anniversaries of the death of a loved one (particularly the first anniversary) are often painful as all the memories surrounding the death and funeral are reawakened. This blessing can be done alone or with others who share your loss. If you do this blessing at home, place a picture(s) of your loved one on the table and, if you have one, a bulletin from the funeral. For option 1, set an unlit candle* next to the picture.
For option 2, set out paper and pencils/pens for all present and an unlit small candle for each person.

WELCOME
For everything there is a season,
and a time for every matter under heaven.
Welcome to this time of remembering (name) and the events surrounding his/her death.

PRAYER
O Lord, on the anniversary of (name)'s death, we come to you for comfort and strength. Heal us of the hurt we are experiencing and the pain of our loss. Give us trust that we are all held in your tender care. Amen

BIBLE TEXT
For I am convinced that neither death, nor life, nor angels,
nor rulers, nor things present, nor things to come, nor powers,
nor height, nor depth, nor anything else in all creation,
will be able to separate us from the love of God
in Christ Jesus our Lord.
Romans 8:38-39

REFLECTION
It is often helpful for people to recount the events surrounding the death and funeral. If you are alone, write in a journal.* If with a group, let all share the events as they experienced them. Or, you may want to focus on events from the loved one's life or share what you miss most.

RITUAL ACTION
OPTION 1 — If you are at the burial place, make the sign of the cross.* If you are at home, light the candle. Then say, *The Lord bless us and keep us. The Lord's face shine on us and be gracious to us. The Lord look upon us with favor, and give us peace.* Amen (Numbers 6: 24-26)

OPTION 2 — Write a letter to your loved one, telling him or her how things are going for you, what parts of your life are still hurting and in what areas healing is happening. As closure to the letter, ask for your loved one's blessing for your new life. Light a small candle claiming that blessing.

If you are gathering with friends or family, you might suggest writing such letters ahead of time. Share as much of your letter as you like with the others.

*For more information see the Introduction.

BLESSING
May I/we find comfort in the new life (name) has with God and in God's faithful love and care for us. Amen

62

SEASONS OF THE CHRISTIAN LIFE

Blessing for Baptismal Anniversaries

PREPARATION Option 1 helps you celebrate the baptismal anniversaries of those who were baptized as infants or small children. Option 2 can be use for celebrating on the day of an adult baptism. Invite family, friends, and baptismal sponsors to celebrate with you. Set a candle* (a baptismal candle or another candle) in the middle of the table to represent Jesus, the *light of the world.* Set one small candle by it for each person present. Place a bowl of water on the table for making the sign of the cross.*

WELCOME
For everything there is a season,
and a time for every matter under heaven.
Welcome to this celebration of our new birth in Christ.

PRAYER
Dear God, thank you for making us part of your family through our baptism into Christ. Help us remember that you dearly love us and want us to trust you each day. Amen

BIBLE TEXT
. . . then he and his entire family were baptized without delay. He brought them up into the house and set food before them; and he and his entire household rejoiced that he had become a believer in God. Acts 16:33b-34

I am the light of the world. Whoever follows me will never walk in darkness but will have the light of life. John 8:12

REFLECTION
OPTION 1 — Tell the child the story of his or her baptismal day — who was there, what you were thinking/feeling on that day. Ask others present who were also there to share their memories. Then tell the stories from your own baptisms.

Finally, share what the baptism of this child meant/means to you.

OPTION 2 — For the one baptized: **What led you to the decision to be baptized? What does it now mean for your life?** Ask others present to share what their own baptisms mean to them, and what your baptism means to them.

RITUAL ACTION
Ask one adult to make the sign of the cross on the forehead of the child or adult, saying,
Remember, (name), you are a child of God.

Light the center candle and say, **Let the light of Christ shine.** Then, have each person light a small candle from the center one and say, **Let Christ's light shine in me.**

SONG
Sing or say, *This Little Light of Mine,* and/or *As You Go on Your Way,* (p. 84), using variation 2.

*For more information see the Introduction.

BLESSING
May the light of Jesus guide us on our paths as we share his love with the world. Amen

Blessing for Entry into Church School

PREPARATION Parents can give Church/Sunday School special importance by doing this blessing prior to the beginning of the Church School year. Place a bowl of water in the center of a table for making the sign of the cross.*

WELCOME
For everything there is a season,
and a time for every matter under heaven.
Welcome as we prepare for this time of learning the stories of God's love.

PRAYER
Dear Lord Jesus, you have asked us to grow in our faith through worship and service, Bible reading and learning. May this Church School Year provide (name[s]) with the opportunity to grow in your love. Amen

BIBLE TEXT
To you, O Lord, I lift up my soul. Make me to know your ways, O Lord; teach me your paths. Lead me in your truth, and teach me, for you are the God of my salvation; for you I wait all day long.
Psalm 25:1,4-5

REFLECTION
Invite each person to reflect on memories of past Church School experiences, if applicable, and hopes and fears for the coming year.

RITUAL ACTION
The parent(s) makes the sign of the cross on the forehead of all those going to Church School, saying, **Child of God, may your heart be open to learning the love of Jesus.**

SONG
Sing or say,
Jesus loves me, this I know,
for the Bible tells me so.

Little ones to him belong,
they are weak, but he is strong.

Yes, Jesus loves me. Yes, Jesus loves me.
Yes, Jesus loves me. The Bible tells me so.

65

*For more information see the Introduction.

BLESSING
May God, who created us all, open our hearts and minds to the knowledge of Jesus' story and love. Amen

Blessing for Receiving Your First Bible

PREPARATION Invite friends and family to be part of a celebration on the day the child receives his or her first Bible. Open your Bible to Deuteronomy 6:4-9. Fill a blessing cup.*

WELCOME

For everything there is a season,
and a time for every matter under heaven.
Welcome to this time for passing on the faith through the stories of the Bible.

PRAYER

Dear God, in the stories of the Bible you tell us how much you love the world. Help us to treasure our Bibles and use them, finding time each day to read and tell each other the stories of faith. Amen

BIBLE TEXT

Read Deuteronomy 6:4-9 in your new Bible. In this text, Moses is telling the people of Israel to never forget the great actions God has done in saving them from their enemies. The Bible is filled with stories that show us God's love and that teach us how to live, especially the stories of Jesus, God's son. That is why we read the Bible and tell the stories.

REFLECTION

Invite any adults present to tell their favorite Bible story or favorite Bible verse and explain why it is important to them. Then ask the recipient of the Bible and other children present, **What is your favorite story?** If possible, find those stories in the new Bible. Read them and talk about what each story teaches us about God.

RITUAL ACTION

Pass the blessing cup and say to one another, **(Name), God's love is for you.**

SONG

Sing or say,
Jesus loves me, this I know, for the Bible tells me so.
Little ones to him belong, they are weak but he is strong.
Yes, Jesus loves me. Yes, Jesus loves me. Yes, Jesus loves me.
The Bible tells me so.

Ask the children for other favorite church school songs they would like to sing.

*For more information see the Introduction.

BLESSING

May we together discover the love of God as we read the stories of the Bible. Amen

Blessing for First Communion

PREPARATION   In many congregations, children receive their first communion several years before they are confirmed. On the day a young person has received his or her first communion, bring together baptismal sponsors, if available, family, friends, or any other important people in the young person's life. Light a candle* and surround it with as many small candles as there are people present.

WELCOME
For everything there is a season,
and a time for every matter under heaven.
Welcome to this time of remembering and celebrating.

PRAYER
Thank you, Jesus, for all you give us: love, forgiveness, acceptance, family, friends, a church home and especially your presence among us. Amen

BIBLE TEXT
Then he took a loaf of bread, and when he had given thanks, he broke it and gave it to them, saying, "This is my body, which is given for you. Do this in remembrance of me." And he did the same with the cup after supper, saying, "This cup that is poured out for you is the new covenant in my blood."
Luke 22:19-20

Again Jesus spoke to them, saying, "I am the light of the world. Whoever follows me will never walk in darkness but will have the light of life." John 8:12

REFLECTION
As the family of God shares bread and wine together, so this is a time for your family to do some sharing. Use these sentence starters to begin the conversation:

(For the one who received first communion)
The bread and wine tasted like . . .
When I received my first communion I felt . . .
The part of the worship service I liked most was . . .
Something I will always remember about this day is . . .

(For family or others gathered)
What I remember about my first communion is . . .
When (name) received his/her first communion, I felt . . .
Something I will always remember about this day is . . .

RITUAL ACTION
Gather around the table where the candles are located.
Ask the young person to light a small candle from the large candle representing Christ's light. Say in unison,
Thank you, Jesus, for welcoming (name) to the Lord's table.
Let your light in her/him always shine.
Then, as each person lights a small candle, repeat the words,
Let your light always shine in (name).

*For more information see the Introduction.

BLESSING
May the table of Christ nourish us and the light of Christ shine in us. Amen

Blessing for Confirmation

PREPARATION Invite friends and family to be part of a celebration on the day of the young person's confirmation. Light a candle* and fill a blessing cup.*

WELCOME

For everything there is a season,
and a time for every matter under heaven.
Welcome to this time of affirming the Christian faith.

PRAYER

From the beginning, gracious God, you have encouraged our growth in faith and understanding of your will. May this same spirit of growth motivate and encourage (name of confirmand)'s heart to draw still closer to you. May we all be reminded of the baptism that claimed us as your children and your light that shines through us. Amen

BIBLE TEXT

When I was a child, I spoke like a child,
I thought like a child, I reasoned like a child;
when I became an adult, I put an end to childish ways.
1 Corinthians 13:11

REFLECTION

Ask the confirmand to think about one or more of the following ideas and share whatever he or she is comfortable sharing.

I think the difference between being a child and being an adult is . . .

While I was being confirmed I felt . . .

I think the difference this is going to make in my life is . . .

Encourage others present to tell of their confirmation day and share what difference their faith makes in their lives.

RITUAL ACTION

Pass the blessing cup and invite each person to give this or another blessing,
May you continue to grow more like Christ.

*For more information see the Introduction.

BLESSING
May our lives be blessed by the peaceful presence of God the Creator, God the Son, and God the Holy Spirit. Amen

Blessing for Discerning Our Vocation and Other Significant Choices

PREPARATION Our vocation can be a career or a job, a way of life, a task or something else we have the gifts to accomplish. This blessing is for times in life when we are faced with significant choices — choices for which intentionally seeking God's will is particularly important. Set a candle* in the center of a table. Have a piece of paper and pen/pencil available. Option 1 can be done alone. Option 2 encourages reaching out to a trusted friend, mentor or counselor.

WELCOME

For everything there is a season,
and a time for every matter under heaven.
Welcome to this time of discerning God's will for my life.

PRAYER

God of abundance, you have granted me gifts and abilities, choices and possibilities. Please help me be open to your guidance concerning the decision I am to make. Amen

BIBLE TEXT

Now to God who by the power at work within us is able to accomplish abundantly far more than all we can ask or imagine, to God be glory . . . I, therefore . . . beg you to lead a life worthy of the calling to which you have been called . . .
Ephesians 3:20-4:1

REFLECTION

Quiet yourself by doing some deep breathing.*
Focus on God's will for your life.

Write your responses to the sentences that fit your situation:

When I think about the world, I am most passionate about . . .
The activities that bring me the greatest joy are . . .
The possibilities I can see right now are . . .
When I think about choosing _____, I feel . . .
Choosing _____ will affect my life and the lives of others by . . .
If I discern _____ as a vocation, the gifts and talents I have that will be utilized are . . . ; the gifts and talents I have that will not be utilized are . . . Choosing _____ will affect my life and the lives of others by . . .

RITUAL ACTION

OPTION 1 — Light the candle. Place your responses next to the candle and pray this prayer,
Light of the world, I place my options before you, asking you to shed light on this decision. I know that my life is in your hands. Amen

OPTION 2 — Share your responses with trusted friends. Ask for their comments. Conclude by doing option 1.

*For more information see the Introduction.

BLESSING

May God's call resonate deep within me, and may I have the courage to trust God's leading. Amen

Blessing the Discovery of Our Spiritual Gifts

PREPARATION We all have been given spiritual gifts to be used for the common good.
At various points in life, we recognize a gift not previously claimed. This blessing will help you celebrate
the joy of that discovery and can be initiated by the person discovering the gift, a friend, or a spiritual leader.
On a piece of paper, write down the spiritual gifts you have discovered. Set out your paper and a begging bowl.*

WELCOME

For everything there is a season,
and a time for every matter under heaven.
Welcome to this time for celebrating our spiritual gifts.

PRAYER

Gracious Giver of good gifts, thank you for allowing me to
discover the spiritual gifts you have given to me, gifts I was
using even when I was not aware of them as gifts. May I now
work more intentionally to use them in meaningful ways
for furthering the Gospel. Amen

BIBLE TEXT

Now there are varieties of gifts, but the same Spirit;
and there are varieties of services, but the same Lord;
and there are varieties of activities, but it is the same God
who activates all of them in everyone. To each is given the
manifestation of the Spirit for the common good.
1 Corinthians 12:4-7

REFLECTION

Write in a journal* or share about the spiritual gifts you have
recently discovered. How did you discover them? How have
you used them in the past? Then finish these sentences:
When I think about the church/world,
I am passionate about . . .
I can envision using my spiritual gifts in this area by . . .

RITUAL ACTION

OPTION 1 — Hold your begging bowl and say these words:
Lord, in gratitude for the spiritual gifts you have given me,
I hold my empty bowl, asking you to put in it opportunities
for me to use these gifts. Amen

OPTION 2 — Spend some time deep breathing.* Then, put
your paper in your begging bowl and lift it high, offering your
gifts to God. Pray a prayer of your own or this prayer,
Lord, you have given me these spiritual gifts. I now give them
back to you, praying that you would give me, also, ways to use
these gifts.

Finally, make a concrete commitment to contact a church or
other organization to explore opportunities to use your
spiritual gifts for the common good.

*For more information see the Introduction.

BLESSING
May all God's children use the gifts God has given them for the common good. Amen

Blessing for Commitment or Recommitment to Jesus Christ

PREPARATION Many persons, at some time in their adult lives, experience a profound commitment or recommitment to Jesus. If you have had such an experience, ask a Christian friend to lead this blessing to name and celebrate that event. Place a candle,* a cross, a bowl of water, and a Bible on a table.

WELCOME
For everything there is a season,
and a time for every matter under heaven.
Welcome to this time of Christian renewal.

PRAYER
Living and loving God, send now the power of your Holy Spirit to strengthen and encourage the faith of those who are entrusting their lives to you. We place ourselves in the hands of the Savior, your Son, Jesus Christ, our Lord. Amen

BIBLE TEXT
God has told you, O mortal, what is good; and what does the Lord require of you but to do justice, and to love kindness, and to walk humbly with your God. Micah 6:8

I can do all things through Christ who strengthens me.
Philippians 4:13

REFLECTION
Ask the person(s) to share responses to the following statements: **For me to do justice is to . . . For me to love kindness is to . . . For me to walk humbly with God is to . . .**

RITUAL ACTION
The leader, while presenting each of the symbols to the person(s) making the commitment, asks the following questions:

We give you this water, which represents the water of baptism through which Jesus claims us as his own. Do you accept it? If so, say "I do."

We give you this cross to represent Jesus who gave his life for your sake and the sake of the world. Do you accept it? If so, say "I do."

We give you this candle to represent the light of Christ that dispels the darkness of our lives. Do you accept it? If so, say "I do."

We give you this Bible in which the love of God through Christ is revealed. Do you accept it? If so, say "I do."

PRAYER
Invite those present to lay hands on the person's head and pray for the person, concluding with:
We pray that Jesus our Lord and Savior will shower you with love and guide you on your daily journey. Amen

*For more information see the Introduction.

BLESSING
May the love of God the Creator, the grace of Jesus the Redeemer,
and the power of the Holy Spirit be with us all. Amen

Blessing of Closure When Leaving a Congregation or Group

PREPARATION When people leave a congregation or group, it is sometimes with much frustration, sometimes with little feeling, and sometimes with much sadness. This blessing will help ease the emotions of a painful leaving, whether that pain is anger or grief, and send people on their way with God's blessing. For congregational use, it can be done with a small group from the congregation or with the whole congregation, if feasible. Fill a blessing cup.* Make copies of the blessing for all gathered.

WELCOME
For everything there is a season,
and a time for every matter under heaven.
Welcome to this time for reflecting upon our life together and wishing each other God's blessings.

PRAYER
God of every yesterday and every tomorrow, make your presence known to us in this time of letting go and moving on. Wrap us in your love. May the experience of grace during this time we spend together support us in the days and weeks ahead. Amen

BIBLE TEXT
Peace I leave with you; my peace I give to you. I do not give to you as the world gives. Do not let your hearts be troubled, and do not let them be afraid. John 14:27

REFLECTION
Ask the person(s) leaving to respond to one or more of these statements: **I am grateful for . . .**   **I am sad about . . .** **I am leaving now because . . .**

If appropriate, have the persons remaining respond, perhaps by sharing ways they are also sad and grateful.

RITUAL ACTION
Say this litany.
Leader: For the joys shared,
Response: Thank you Lord.
Leader: For the hurts caused,
Response: Forgive us Lord.
Leader: For new beginnings,
Response: Bless us Lord.

Invite people to pass the blessing cup, saying,
May the peace of the Lord be with you.

If the group is large, give the blessing cup to the person(s) leaving to drink, while the others speak the blessing. Those leaving then respond, **And also with you.**

*For more information see the Introduction.

BLESSING
Sing or say the blessing song, *As You Go on Your Way,* (p. 84).

Blessing for Times of Struggle, Doubt, and Despair

PREPARATION Set a cross, a picture, nails or other images of Jesus' suffering in the center of a table with a large, lit candle.* Surround them with small unlit candles. Turn off the lights.

WELCOME

For everything there is a season,
and a time for every matter under heaven.
This is a time for remembering I am not alone.

PRAYER

O God of darkness as well as light, of night as well as day,
be with me and guide me during this dark time, for "even the
darkness is not dark to you" (Psalm 139:12). Amen

BIBLE TEXT

My God, my God, why have you forsaken me? Why are you
so far from helping me, from the words of my groaning?
Psalm 22:1

REFLECTION

Consider the writer of the verse, living over three thousand years ago, who wrote of being forsaken by God. Then think about Jesus, who memorized this verse at some point in his life and spoke it from the cross (Matthew 27:46). Look at the images or symbols of Jesus' suffering. Imagine his struggle, doubt and despair. Consider these two people, the writer and Jesus, as your companions during this dark time. Speak your despair to your companions.

RITUAL ACTION

OPTION 1 — Pray these prayers, and as you finish each prayer, light a small candle.

Jesus, I struggle with . . .
Jesus, I doubt that . . .
Jesus, I despair about . . .

When completed conclude with,
Jesus, into your hands I commend my spirit (Luke 23:46).

OPTION 2 — Pray the prayers suggested in option 1 and light candles for each prayer. When you have finished, relax in this room with many flickering lights. Begin deep breathing.* Whisper the phrase over and over again,
Into your hands, as you breathe in, and
I commend my spirit, as you breathe out.

Give to Jesus your spirit of despair.

Turn on lights in the room before blowing out the candles.

*For more information see the Introduction.

BLESSING
May Jesus, my companion in dark times, be also my companion in joy. Amen

Blessing for Protection against Evil

PREPARATION This blessing can be done by the person desiring protection from evil or by others for that person. Though this blessing can be done alone, it is recommended that spiritual friends, mentors, or pastors be present. In preparation for the blessing, take much time praying confessional prayers, claiming Christ's victory over evil and rejoicing in Christ's unconditional love for all people. Place a lit candle* and a bowl of water or oil on a table for making the sign of the cross.*

WELCOME
For everything there is a season,
and a time for every matter under heaven.
This is a time of intercession for safety and protection from the forces of evil.

PRAYER
Dear Jesus Christ our Lord, you entered into death to claim victory over the evil one. I/We pray now as you taught us, "Deliver us from evil." Amen

BIBLE TEXT
Put on the whole armor of God, so that you may be able to stand against the wiles of the devil. For our struggle is not against enemies of blood and flesh, but against the rulers, against the authorities, against the cosmic powers of this present darkness, against the spiritual forces of evil in the heavenly places. Ephesians 6:11-12

REFLECTION
Have the person asking for intercession share or write in a journal* why he or she is asking for protection from evil, his or her thoughts and feelings concerning evil, and, if appropriate, his or her encounter with evil.

Invite those gathered to share their thoughts and feelings and give appropriate feedback.

RITUAL ACTION
Make the sign of the cross on the forehead of those asking for protection. Say, **In the name of Jesus and by his shed blood, I declare victory over the power of evil. Nothing can separate us from the love of God in Christ Jesus. Amen**

PRAYER
(If praying for another, lay hands on him or her and replace "me" with his or her name in the prayer.)
Claiming my status as a beloved child of God, I pray: Jesus, our Redeemer and Lord, dress me in the whole armor of God. Give me a breast plate of love to protect my heart from fear. Give me sturdy shoes that I may walk over sharp stones and not be hurt. Give me a helmet, shining with your power, deflecting the insidious wiles of the evil one from entering my thoughts and feelings. And finally, wrap me in the light of your Holy Spirit, a light so powerful that no evil can enter. Amen

*For more information see the Introduction.

BLESSING
May the love of God surround us. May the peace of Jesus live within.
May the power of the Spirit give us discernment and protection. Amen

Seasons of the Church Year

Blessing for Advent

PREPARATION The season of Advent begins on the Sunday closest to the 28th of November and lasts for approximately four weeks until Christmas. Traditionally, it has been a time of quiet and preparation, a time when we make ourselves ready to receive Jesus into our hearts and lives at Christmas. More and more Christians are finding the intentional celebration of Advent a way of minimizing the stress and hyper-activity of our culture during those pre-Christmas weeks. Creating Advent rituals can be particularly effective for children, helping them look forward with quiet anticipation to the coming of Christ at Christmas. You could begin with one or two parts of the blessing and then add more each year. Also, incorporate this blessing into your Christmas Eve/Day celebrations. If possible, place a blue cloth on a table and on it an Advent wreath (circular candle holder) or log with four blue candles,* a nativity scene with moveable characters so you can move Mary and Joseph one step closer to the manger each day of Advent, and a Bible. For option 2 you will need a begging bowl.* Light one new candle for every Sunday in Advent. Do this blessing every night during Advent or as many nights as possible. Setting a tone of anticipation and mystery is particularly important for this blessing, so dim the lights and turn off the phone and TV. Remember to invite, never coerce, family members to be part of this blessing.

WELCOME
For everything there is a season,
and a time for every matter under heaven.
Welcome to this Advent season of hope and expectation.

SONGS
Throughout the season, you are encouraged to learn Advent songs, singing as many as you wish every night, both before and after the reflection.
(See your church hymnals for suggestions.)

BIBLE TEXT
On each night of the season, read one of the passages listed on p.83.

REFLECTION
Share or journal* about some or all of the following thoughts. If you are celebrating Advent with children, accept with delight and good humor all their responses.
The words or phrase that I remember from the text are . . .
I think I remember those words because . . .
They remind me of . . .   God might be trying to tell me . . .

PRAYER
OPTION 1 — Pray the squeeze prayer* or a prayer of your own. Close with the Lord's Prayer (p. 84).

OPTION 2 — Spend time deep breathing.* Then hold the begging bowl, asking God to give you what you need to prepare your heart for Christmas.

*For more information see the Introduction.

BLESSING
May the God of hope be with us, preparing us for the coming of Jesus. Amen

Blessing for The Twelve Days of Christmas

PREPARATION Many families carry on family traditions on Christmas Eve and Day. Create sacred traditions for those days, including reading the Christmas story (Luke 2:1-20), singing Christmas carols, and praying. This blessing will help you extend the holiness of the season and stretch the concept of gift giving to the giving of non-material gifts. If possible, place a white cloth on a table and on it one tall candle* representing the Christ child and twelve small candles. Light one for each day of Christmas (one the first day, two the second . . .). If you have a nativity scene, arrange this on the cloth as well. It is helpful to dim the lights and turn off the phone and TV to create a quiet, holy space. This blessing can be done on each of the twelve days of Christmas.

Some families choose to give a gift on each day of Christmas rather than sharing all gifts on Christmas Eve or Day. During this season, you are encouraged to give non-material GIFTS (God Isn't Found in Things) like a poem, a song, a drawing, a hug, an affirmation, a prayer, a "thank you," an "I'm sorry," a promise, an offer to help . . .

WELCOME
For everything there is a season,
and a time for every matter under heaven.
Welcome to this Christmas season, a time for celebrating the gift of Jesus.

SONGS
You are encouraged to learn Christmas carols, singing as many as you wish both before and after the reflection and ritual action. (See your church hymnals for suggestions.)

BIBLE TEXT
. . . the fruit of the Spirit is love, joy, peace, patience, kindness, generosity, faithfulness, gentleness, and self-control. There is no law against such things. Galatians 5:22-23

And now faith, hope, and love abide, these three; and the greatest of these is love. 1 Corinthians 13:13

REFLECTION
Each night of the Twelve Days of Christmas, choose one of the gifts or fruits of the Spirit mentioned in the text to talk about or write about in a journal,*asking,
How can I share or show the gift of ___ with others in my daily life? Be as specific as possible, especially if children are participating.

RITUAL ACTION
Share one of the GIFTS listed above or another non-material gift. If you are also giving presents, share them.

PRAYER
Pray the squeeze prayer* or a prayer of your own. Close with the Lord's Prayer (p. 84).

*For more information see the Introduction.

BLESSING
Giver of all good GIFTS, fill our hearts with gratitude and joy. Amen

Blessing for Epiphany

PREPARATION Epiphany is both a day and a season. Epiphany (January 6) is the celebration of the arrival in Bethlehem of the Magi (or Wise Men from the East), led by a star, bringing Jesus precious gifts. The season of Epiphany extends until Lent, approximately two months. On a table, place a large candle,* representing the star of Bethlehem, and around it a small candle for each person. You will also need a Bible. Light the large candle.

WELCOME
For everything there is a season,
and a time for every matter under heaven.
Welcome to this Epiphany season.

SONGS
Throughout the season, you are encouraged to learn Epiphany songs, singing as many as you wish both before and after the reflection and ritual action. (See your church hymnals for suggestions.)

BIBLE TEXT
The Epiphany Story: Matthew 2:1-12

REFLECTION
The three visitors from the East brought Jesus, the child of poor parents, valuable gifts. Share or write in a journal* about what you think might be a comparable gift today, and then finish the following sentences:
In our culture, the material things people value most are . . . (clothes, cars . . .). The material things I value most are . . . In our culture, the non-material things people value most are . . . (friendship, health, generosity . . .). The non-material things I value most are . . .

RITUAL ACTION
One at a time, light your small candle from the large candle, saying, **May the star lead me to Jesus today.**

In Matthew 25:40, Jesus tells us,
". . . just as you did it to one of the least of these who are members of my family, you did it to me."

During the Epiphany season, commit yourself to an intentional way of bringing valuable gifts to Jesus, whose face we see in people who have needs. Consider giving time at a soup kitchen, nursing home, prison, shelter or other such organization or setting. You can also give money to a number of worthwhile charities.

PRAYER
Pray the squeeze prayer* or a prayer of your own. Close with the Lord's Prayer (p. 84). Be sure to include prayers for people in need.

*For more information see the Introduction.

BLESSING
May the God of "the least of these" give us open hearts and generous hands. Amen

Blessing for Lent

PREPARATION Lent, the season before Easter, has traditionally been set aside for preparation of the soul for the death and resurrection of Jesus. That preparation often takes the form of various disciplines--fasting, prayer, confession, asking forgiveness, attendance at special worship services. You are encouraged to adopt a discipline during this Lenten season. Make this blessing a part of that discipline by doing it every night during Lent or as many nights as possible. Setting a tone of quiet mystery is particularly important, so dim the lights and turn off the phone and TV. Remember to invite, never coerce, family members to be part of this blessing. If possible, place a purple cloth on a table and on it six purple candles (one for each week of Lent). Also, set out a Bible and, for option 2, a begging bowl.* At the beginning of Lent, you may also wish to plant seeds in pots that will bloom in about six weeks. Place these plants on the table as well.

WELCOME
For everything there is a season,
and a time for every matter under heaven.
Welcome to this Lenten season of quiet growth and mystery.

SONGS
Throughout the season, you are encouraged to learn Lenten songs, singing as many as you wish every night, both before and after the reflection.
(See your church hymnals for suggestions.)

BIBLE TEXT
On each night of the Lenten season, read one of the passages listed on p. 83.

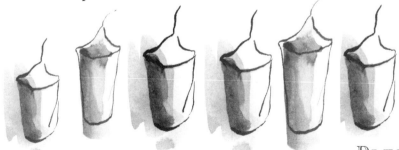

REFLECTION
Share or write in a journal* about these questions. If you are celebrating with children, accept with delight and good humor all their responses.
Why do you think Jesus did this or told this story?
What can I learn from this story?
How does this story help me grow as a Christian?

If you have adopted other disciplines, take time to share or write in a journal* about how your disciplines are going and how you are growing in faith through them.

PRAYER
OPTION 1 — Pray the squeeze prayer* or a prayer of your own. Close with the Lord's Prayer (p. 84).

OPTION 2 — Spend time deep breathing.* Then hold the begging bowl, asking God to give you those experiences, whether painful or joyful, you need to grow in your relationship with Jesus.

*For more information see the Introduction.

BLESSING
May our gracious and loving God walk with us during this time of mystery and growth. Amen

Blessing for Easter

PREPARATION Easter is both a day and a season in which we celebrate Christ's resurrection and the promise of eternal life. We also celebrate the possibility that we can be raised out of the dead places in our lives now and given new life. The season begins on Easter Sunday and lasts until Pentecost. If possible, place a white or gold cloth on a table, and on it symbols of new life (spring plants, lilies, eggs . . .). You will also need a Bible. For option 1, fill a blessing cup,* and for option 2, set out a begging bowl.*

WELCOME
For everything there is a season,
and a time for every matter under heaven.
Welcome to this season for celebrating resurrected life!

SONGS
Throughout the season, you are encouraged to learn Easter songs, singing as many as you wish both before and after the reflection/ritual action.
(See your church hymnals for suggestions.)

BIBLE TEXT
Read one of the Easter stories: Matthew 28:1-10, Mark 16:1-8, Luke 24:1-12, or John 20:1-18.

REFLECTION/RITUAL ACTION
OPTION 1 — Share or write in a journal* about a time in your life when you felt particularly sad, bad, or even dead inside (times of despair or no feelings at all). How did God help you through those times? Was it through a person? A song? An event? The Bible? . . . Was it through belief in the certainty of resurrection and eternal life? Then pass the blessing cup, saying, **Thank you, God, for hope and joy and for the promise of new life.**

OPTION 2 — Psalm 30:5 says, *Weeping may linger for the night, but joy comes with the morning.*

Share or write in a journal* about yourself or someone you know who has gone through a period of suffering but found new life. Then ask,
Are there places of deadness in my own life now?
(for instance, despair, grief, sickness, addiction, loneliness, buried anger or resentment).
Spend some time deep breathing.* Then hold the begging bowl, saying, **God, fill me with hope that you can and will raise me to new life.**

Jesus could not raise himself. He was raised from the dead by God. Neither can we raise ourselves out of our dead places. The Spirit of God works through others to help us. During this Easter season, commit yourself to thanking those people who have helped you during difficult times. Also, seek out others who might need your help.

PRAYER
Pray the squeeze prayer* or a prayer of your own.
Close with the Lord's Prayer (p. 84).

*For more information see the Introduction.

BLESSING
May God raise us out of our dead places and into the joy of new life. Amen

Blessing for Pentecost

PREPARATION Pentecost is both a day and a season, extending from the Day of Pentecost (usually in early June) until Advent. It is a time for claiming the power of the Holy Spirit for our daily living to help us grow in faith and courage and love. If possible, place a red cloth and a single red candle* on a table, along with a small candle for each person. You will also need a Bible and, for option 2, a begging bowl.* Light the red candle.

WELCOME
For everything there is a season,
and a time for every matter under heaven.
Welcome to this day for inspiring courage.

SONGS
You are encouraged to learn Pentecost songs, singing as many as you wish both before and after the reflection/ritual action. (See your church hymnals for suggestions.)

BIBLE TEXT
Read the Pentecost Story:
Acts 2:1-24, 37-47. This is a story of an experience that turned timid, frightened men and women into bold people — people who could tell the world that Jesus rose from the dead, people who could tell their own story about how the teachings of Jesus and the coming of the Holy Spirit changed their lives.

REFLECTION/RITUAL ACTION
OPTION 1 — It takes courage to show Christ's love in word and deed to others. Share or write in a journal* about how, where, or with whom you want to show the love of Jesus more boldly. Then light your small candle from the center candle, saying, **Holy Spirit, fill me with courage to show Christ's love.**

OPTION 2 — Share or write in a journal* about a time when you were afraid and God gave you both the courage and the ability to do or say something important. Then share or write in a journal about a current situation in which you need the courage to say or do something important. What are your fears about it? What keeps you from acting boldly? Then, holding your begging bowl, spend some time deep breathing.*

When you are through, pray these words or a prayer of your own: **Spirit of the Living God, fill me with courage to boldly say and do what you desire.** Finally, light a candle, claiming the presence of the Holy Spirit in your life.

PRAYER
Pray the squeeze prayer* or a prayer of your own. Close with the Lord's Prayer (p. 84).

*For more information see the Introduction.

BLESSING
May the Holy Spirit of courage and power be with all who call Jesus, "Lord." Amen

BIBLE TEXTS FOR ADVENT

These Bible passages are based on the Advent themes of God's promise, preparation to receive the promise, waiting in hope for the promise, and the fulfillment of God's promise. There are seven texts for each week. Read one each day.

Week 1--The Promise
First Sunday: Luke 1:26-38; Isaiah 11:1-5; Isaiah 11:6-10; Jeremiah 31:16-17, 31-34; Isaiah 2:2-5; Isaiah 35:1-10; Jeremiah 33:14-15

Week 2--The Preparation
Second Sunday: Luke 1:57-80; Luke 3:1-6; Romans 13:11-14; Isaiah 40:1-9; Luke 3:10-14; Romans 12:1-2; 1 Thessalonians 5:16-24

Week 3--The Waiting
Third Sunday: Luke 1:39-45; James 5:7-11; Lamentations 3:21-26; Romans 8:18-28; 2 Peter 3:8-15a; Psalm 27; Psalm 42

Week 4--The Promise Fulfilled
Fourth Sunday: Luke 1:46-55; Micah 5:2-5a; Luke 4:15-21; 1 Samuel 2:1-10; Isaiah 9:6-7; Psalm 85:8-13; Psalm 146:5-10

Christmas Eve or Day: Luke 2:1-20

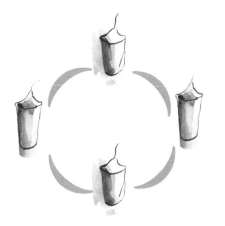

BIBLE TEXTS FOR LENT

These Bible passages present highlights from Jesus' teachings and ministry. They lead the reader to a deeper appreciation of the sadness of the Holy Week events and the power of the Easter message. Read one text each day.

Jesus' Ministry Begins
Ash Wednesday: Matthew 3:13 - 4:11; Luke 5:1-11; Matthew 5:1-12 and Luke 6:20-26; Matthew 5:13-16

Week 1--Teachings of Jesus
First Sunday: Luke 10:25-37; Matthew 22:34-40; Luke 6:31-42; Luke 12:22-34; Mark 4:35-41; Luke 11:1-4 and Matthew 6:9-13; Mark 12:38-44

Week 2--Healing Stories
Second Sunday: Matthew 15:21-28; Mark 2:1-5; Luke 13:10-17; Luke 17:11-19; Mark 5:25-34; John 11:17-44; Mark 10:46-52

Week 3--What is God Like?
Third Sunday: Luke 15:11-32; Luke 15:1-10; Luke 13:34; Luke 18:1-8; Matthew 7:7-11; Matthew 13:31-33; John 10:11-15

Week 4--Models of Discipleship
Fourth Sunday: John 4:5-15, 25-30, 39; John 15:1-11; Mark 4:1-9, 13-20; Luke 10:38-42; Matthew 7:24-27; John 6:1-14; Matthew 16:21-26

Week 5--The Challenge of Discipleship
Fifth Sunday: Matthew 17:1-8; Mark 9:33-37 and 10:13-16; Matthew 19:16-26; Luke 14:12-24; Luke 12:13-21; Luke 16:19-31; Matthew 25:34-45

Week 6--Holy Week
Palm Sunday: Mark 11:1-10; Mark 11:15-18; Mark 14:1-31; Mark 14:32-46; Mark 14:66-72; Mark 15:1-41; Mark 15:42-47

Easter Sunday: Luke 24:1-12

THE LORD'S PRAYER

Our Father in heaven,
hallowed be your name,
your kingdom come,
your will be done,
   on earth as in heaven.
Give us today our daily bread.
Forgive us our sins
as we forgive those
   who sin against us.
Save us from the time of trial
   and deliver us from evil.
For the kingdom, the power, and the glory
   are yours, now and forever.
   Amen

THE AARONIC BENEDICTION

The Lord bless you and keep you.
The Lord's face shine on you
   and be gracious to you.
The Lord look upon you with favor
   and give you peace.
   Amen (Numbers 6: 24-26)

THE SERENITY PRAYER

God, grant me the serenity
to accept the things I cannot change,
courage to change the things I can,
and wisdom to know the difference.
   Amen (anonymous)

As You Go On Your Way

Anonymous   John Ylvisaker

Variation 1. As I go on my way may Christ go with me, etc.
Variation 2. As we go on our way may Christ go with us, etc.